i

Wake Up, Wise Up, Win!

WAKE UP,

WISE UP,

WIN!

By

L.F. "Bill" Zimmermann

This book is dedicated to Miriam S. Zimmermann and to the memory of her late husband, and my father, John A. Zimmermann, Sr., two happy and successful people.

First Edition
Edited by C.R. Neil and Sandra S. Chaisson
Designed by Stephanie Stephens

Zimmermann, L.F. "Bill" (Lawrence F.)
    Wake Up, Wise Up, Win! / L.F. "Bill" Zimmermann
    p.cm
    Includes index
    ISBN: 0-9653145-5-3

    1.   Self-help techniques
    2.   Motivation (Psychology)
    3.   Happiness
        I. Title

    BF 632.z56 1998   158.1
    QBI98.174

    Second Edition ISBN: 978-0965314558

ACKNOWLEDGMENTS

There are so many people who have contributed to the writing of this book that it is impossible to thank each of them individually.

I especially wish to thank Brenda Lambert Zimmermann, my loving and patient wife, for her help with numerous proof-readings, her encouragement, and for all of the time she spent alone while I was busy at the computer.

My gratitude also goes out to Philip D. Carter, Dan T. Manget, Avis R. Moore and Carol M. Moses, friends who have made my recent years so enjoyable.

Finally, I would like to thank all of my family and friends who have helped me achieve my goals, in both my personal and business endeavors.

I truly believe that those who have gone on to a greater happiness in the hereafter understand the great love and gratitude that I have for them, and know that I will always remember the vital part that they played in my life.

One of the by-products of being a Super Bowl winning coach is that many people send me books to review. While I don't have time to read them all, *Wake Up, Wise Up, Win* caught my attention. The message is forceful. The message is essential. The message is truth.

As a professional football coach, I have found that, in order to win consistently, it takes players with outstanding character and the ability to be a true team player. In my play book, character beats talent any day of the week. Raw talent alone is not the answer to winning. Coaching a professional football team, just like managing any other type of business, requires team members who are honest, hard working and compatible.

The "hot dog" runs 80 yards for a touchdown and "dances" in the end zone for the camera. A *team* player runs the same 80 yards, with the same results, but celebrates in the end zone with his teammates who successfully cleared the way. No effort is singular. The celebration that follows a good, hard run should involve as many players as the play took to complete. A person who can share the glory of accomplishment with those who assisted in making the task become a reality is a person of strong character. Understanding that no one accomplishes anything totally alone in a sign of strength, not of weakness — the same is true in business and in life.

Throughout Wake Up, Wise Up, Win! Bill Zimmermann emphasizes personal self-esteem and the commitment to serving others for a common good. This is truly the formula for success.

Coach Mike Ditka

New Orleans Saints

Win or Lose

by

L.F. "Bill" Zimmermann

I saw a young man all alone yesterday,
with his head hanging down, deep in thoughts of dismay.
"What's wrong with me?" he did softly sigh.
"My life is so bad I sure wish I would die".
His whole face was drawn, and his voice full of fear.
His sad eyes were strained, and ready to tear.
I said, "Don't be so sad, and surely don't fret.
Life is too short to be filled with regret.
Forget your sad past. Start fresh with today.
Don't accept a dull life of all work and no play.
It's not what you have, and not who you know,
it's your spirit within and the good that you sow
The time has now come, and I ask you to see,
there's true happiness here for both you and me.
Just ponder this question, while singing your blues:
Why do winners win, and why do losers lose'?
Winners it seems, play out every hand.
They keep on keeping on, and think life is grand.
Losers lose hope, and they give up on life.
They don't love themselves, and have days full of strife.
But, it's a matter of choice. That's all that is takes.
Learn to love yourself first. See the difference it makes.
When you loving you becomes step number one,
you'll soon find serving others can be lots of fun.
So what will it be? What life will you choose?
Will you choose to win, or will you choose to lose?"
The young man thought long, and agreed by reply:
"What good would it do if I were to die.
Instead of a life full of grief and self-pity,
I'll simply have fun, and even be witty.
I'll face life anew, and I'll lift up my chin.
I'll have faith in the truth, and I'll choose to win."

ABOUT THE AUTHOR

Lawrence F. "Bill" Zimmermann is the last of seven children. At last count, he and Brenda, his wife of twenty-six years, have five living children, 25 grandchildren, and two great-grandchildren between them. Brenda's oldest daughter died on January 3, 2008.

Ever since winning every subscription drive in his newspaper delivery district at the age of 13, Bill has achieved numerous leadership roles, simply by following his father's example of providing service and letting others do their thing.

After graduating from Louisiana State University, he served as a pilot and flight instructor in the U.S. Air Force. He received an MBA from the University of New Orleans and his Doctor of Business Administration Degree from Grenoble Ecole de Management in France. He has specialized in management troubleshooting and business turnarounds. He also owned his own real estate management and construction companies since 1965.

An Adjunct Professor of Business Management, he is currently on the faculty of University of Phoenix, DeVry University, Central Michigan University and Concordia University. He was previously the Chair for Undergraduate Business and Management at the Louisiana Campus of the University of Phoenix.

He is a member of the American Society for Training and Development, The Southern Management Association, and the U.S. Defense Department's Employer in Support of the Guard and Reserve Committee. He has published two additional books and a number of magazine articles. He has been listed in Who's Who in Professional Speaking,

ABOUT THE BOOK

Beginning with the introduction and through to the final chapter, this book takes you along a natural evolution of leadership, building on the theme of individual happiness and fulfillment as being the key ingredients for true success in all human relationships, especially in working with others to accomplish your goals in the business world.

Each chapter builds on the points made in the previous chapters, and the book culminates with a practical discussion of teamwork. The final chapter of the book takes in to account and reinforces the importance of all of the propositions brought out in first twelve chapters.

The book is primarily written to be read straight through for enjoyment and self-satisfaction. For the serious student of leadership and management, all of the key words and phrases to remember are printed in bold type. The author presents his content filled **TIMELESS TIPS** throughout the book.

A key word index which provides an easy means of finding the primary location of key topics for further review is included at the back of the book, along with a suggested reading list.

Chapter	Title	Page
1	The Fame Game *(Making Choices)*	1
2	Baby Steps *(Fundamentals)*	27
3	In Control *(Leadership Roles)*	43
4	Can I Help *(Providing Service)*	57
5	Get A Life *(Self-confidence)*	79
6	Yes or No *(Communications)*	93
7	Dialogue Direction *(Responsibility)*	107
8	Dreaming and Scheming *(Goals)*	133
9	First Things First *(Planning)*	147
10	Sunrise *(Facing Change)*	167
11	In the Army *(Empowerment)*	199
12	Cleared For Solo *(Relationships)*	213
13	Go Team Go *(Teamwork)*	229
	Key Word Index	255

Introduction

Some people are born into money and fame, but for most of us, the only way we can meet our basic needs is through our own talents and efforts. In other words, most of us have to work to earn a living.

While making money certainly isn't everything, for most of the billions of people like me on this earth, reality dictates that we still have to work hard every day.

No matter what kind of talents you have, there are two principal ways to make the most of them in the working world: 1) Be in business for yourself, or 2) Rise through the ranks of management.

This book is dedicated to those legions of hard working people who find their role in life pursuing business ownership or organizational management as their ticket to a lifetime of financial stability.

It's a book especially for those who feel they are frantically going through life on a run-a-way carnival carousel, going round and round in endless circles, never getting anywhere, yet they can't get off. That's one wooden pony ride that can easily become hell-on-earth if you can't stop listening to the same old deadly dirge of that morbid merry-go-round of unhappiness. It's the music of pessimists and cynics.

The older I get, the more I'm convinced that striving for fame and fortune is a totally frustrating and futile activity.

Moreover, fame and fortune are forever fickle and most often very fleeting affairs.

The most perplexing questions about worldly success are eternally unanswerable: How much is enough? How long will fame last?

Being in a state of healthy mental happiness is really what success is all about. It's what all people are looking for, whether they realize it or not.

Here's the problem: Most unhappy people don't know why they're not happy, and they don't understand that happiness is strictly an intellectual choice, which brings on an emotional response. Happiness is not the result of public achievement.

This book was written for the multitude of good people bending under the relentless pressure of trying to be some **"thing"** special, instead of being happy being some **"one"** special. **"What you do" is not nearly as important as "who you are"!**

Choosing to be happy is a decision you can make at any time. Yet, the gift of instant happiness, which is ours free for the taking, simply eludes many of us.

In actuality, finding true happiness and success is simply accepting the blissful joy of a contented and peaceful state of mind. Just be happy! That's all it takes. No more, no less.

Like most people, I've gone through some really rough times in my life, both emotional and financial. Isn't it strange how those two insidious blood pressure elevators always seem to go together?

There were times when I paid much too much attention to my own egocentric selfish goals, at the expense of everybody else; instead of finding the endless joy and lasting satisfaction in simply meeting the normal challenges of daily life.

There were other times, when my own needs didn't count at all. Like the times that I thought that I was responsible for taking care of everything, for everybody. In hindsight, those times were the worst of times!

Like most entrepreneurs, I've also learned some very tough and expensive lessons in my business life. Luckily, I haven't had to keep on learning the same lessons over and over again. Tuition isn't cheap when you keep repeating courses at the "University of Hard Knocks. "

I've heard many of the things in this book preached up and down the street for most of my life. Most of them are probably in the "public domain", but if I fail to give the proper credit for something that someone else said before me, please don't take offense. I probably just don't know where I heard or read it for the first time. I don't really want to take the credit for something I didn't make up.

The only thing that matters to me is that you get some enjoyment and personal satisfaction from reading my book, and that you will use the many ideas and *Timeless Tips* to your benefit. They absolutely work!

I think you'll quickly recognize much of the advice in this book as a handy collection of good old common sense adages and sound management ideas. Some may sound like yesterday's news, but the marvelous thing is that they really work!

The people that reviewed this book told me that they thought it was great. But, they all know and love me, and there is a very slight chance that they only told me what they thought I wanted to hear. I do hope you enjoy my book, and I do hope you embrace its true spirit.

I've been successfully using these ideas for most of my life, and I put them in this book because I am absolutely convinced that they'll work for you too. What's more, I promise that if you truly believe they'll work, they most certainly will.

After a lifetime of searching, I realize that I've truly found the one straight path to a little bit of heaven right here on earth. Admittedly, it has taken me a few years, but I finally understand this simple, yet most basic, secret of life:

Happiness
Is
Success!

CHAPTER 1

"The Fame Game"

What is success worth?

People who lack self-confidence usually get their priorities all mixed up. They place the sequence of happiness and success backwards, and many times they make the wrong choices.

This true life story of my old boyhood friend, Kenny, illustrates my firm beliefs about happiness and success better than any story I could possibly make up.

I met Kenny in June of 1945; right after World War II had ended. My father had just re-married after being a widower for eight years. Shortly before their wedding, Daddy and my step-mother, Mimi, had just bought their first house.

Kenny was my new next door neighbor. Kenny and I were direct opposites in most ways. I was the last of seven children, and Kenny an only child. I was nine. He was seven. I was active, and he was passive. I was the typical skinny little kid, and Kenny was somewhat on the chubby side. He reminded me of Spanky of the "Our Gang" movies.

We lived in the stately old tree-lined University section of New Orleans, only two blocks away from the picturesque Audubon Park.

The park provided endless free entertainment, and it was the kind of super playground that any normally active young boy would treasure.

There was plenty of open space for football and baseball, and the park's peacefully shady lagoons were full of ducks and geese, and were great for fishing.

Outfitted with a short length of black sewing thread, a tiny hook, and a slice of bread, we could catch all the sun perch we wanted to. Usually, fishing only cost two-bits for a fishing permit.

On some days we were lucky, those were the days when we caught our limit of fish and left the park before the fishing permit seller came around.

There were some wonderful old amusement rides in the park in those days. There was always fun on the carousel, and the graceful "Swan Boat" majestically plied the winding lagoons. The gigantic Olympic-sized, double swimming pool was always an exciting place to pass time in the summer. Even the aging Audubon Park Zoo was great fun, and the admission was free. Many forms of public entertainment were still free in those good old days.

Kenny lived in a big, old, three-story house, which had been remodeled in to what we called an apartment house. He lived in the lower front apartment.

A middle-aged single lady who gave refuge to at least twenty stray cats lived in one of the rear apartments. In those days most people would thoughtlessly describe her as an "Old Maid." Most of the kids in the neighborhood called her the "Cat Lady."

Kenny loved those cats, but whenever his mother saw one of them around she would chase it away. His mother never wanted him to play with animals, and having a pet of his own was strictly taboo. I always felt a little sorry for Kenny, because I knew he longed for a pet of his own.

Kenny's apartment had a small front room that had been converted from a covered front porch. Most of the space in this little parlor was taken up by a piano and a small sofa.

There was a slightly larger dining room connected to the parlor, and a very tiny efficiency kitchen off of the dining room.

A few years ago, I learned that the rest of the apartment consisted of only one bedroom and one bath. As a child, I never saw that hidden bedroom and bath. They were always closed off behind two massive and mysterious sliding pocket doors.

Kenny's mother was an elocution teacher. In those days, more kindly people would describe her outward appearance as prim and stylishly stout.

She was a very proud lady. She considered herself an aristocrat, a true southern lady. She sincerely thought that she was a better person than the ordinary people around her. She often implied as much, while correcting my many errors in speech.

3

Even though I was young, I knew that she was determined to create an air of elegance and respect about herself. She longed for respect and adulation.

To this day, I still don't know why Kenny's mother allowed him to be friends with me.

Perhaps it was abundantly evident at least to her, that when it came to talent and intelligence, I was certainly no competition for Kenny. I guess I wasn't a threat.

I think I was Kenny's only real friend in the neighborhood. Yet, I clearly understood, that in his mother's vision of the world, I was definitely a member of the unfortunate and uncultured mass of humanity.

Kenny's father was a "Buick" salesman. To us kids, he was a real success. We thought he was rich.

It was right after the war, and he drove the only brand new car in the neighborhood. We didn't know it wasn't his new car.

When Kenny's dad came home from work he would park his new Buick demonstrator at the curb, and immediately go into his apartment. He never spent any time playing outside with Kenny, as some of the other kids' fathers would occasionally do.

During those strange times when I was visiting inside of Kenny's house, the two huge sliding bedroom doors were always closed. Even though Kenny's father might be home while I was there, I never once saw him come out of his room. Whenever I was in his apartment, his mother was always right with us, but never his dad. We were never left alone.

Even as a child, I could see that there was an icy estrangement between Kenny's mother and father. Kenny's dad maintained this self-imposed exile each time I was there. Evidently, all three of them slept in the same bedroom.

His father would always tell me hello on his way into the house. He always seemed like a very nice man.

I got the strong impression that his father had little input into Kenny's upbringing, although not by his choice.

I only remember one occasion when Kenny's dad attempted to have any influence on his son's boyhood image. I think he had just bought a new camera, and he asked me and one of my other friends, Benny, to let him take a picture of us standing next to Kenny.

The two of us had been playing football in the school yard, and his dad asked us to let Kenny hold the football while he took a picture of us all standing together.

While it was a vain attempt at implanting at least some type of male bonding image into Kenny's childhood memories, it is an interesting and revealing photo.

We were in our old play clothes, and Kenny was standing next to us holding the football, wearing pressed dress pants, dress shirt, knit sweater, and tweed sport coat with a handkerchief in the pocket, polished dress shoes, and his hair perfectly combed.

After he took the snapshot, Kenny's dad once again went inside to his place of exile. He didn't even stay out to be with Kenny on that day. When a few minutes had passed, Kenny's mother ordered Kenny to come in the house.

5

While I was only allowed to be in his parlor and dining room, to the best of my knowledge, I was one of the very few children on the block who was ever welcomed inside of Kenny's apartment. At least I don't ever remember anyone else being there at the same time I was.

Our two houses were right across the street from LaSalle Grammar School.

The public school had a large fenced in play area where most of us kids in the neighborhood played daily.

Even though we went to several different schools, all the kids, except Kenny, played there after school together for hours and hours, almost every day. We usually stayed outside right up until supper time, not wanting to waste any precious play time.

During the summer recess, we would jump the fence because the gate was locked. We would play in the school yard until Mr. Murphy, the caretaker, chased us out. If we weren't in the school yard, we were in the park. All of us except, Kenny.

I don't remember Kenny ever being allowed to play in the school yard with the other kids, and he never went with us to the park. Kenny's mother never let him stay outside after school for very long while school was in session.

Occasionally, his mother did let him stay out just to talk to me for a short time. We would either sit on my front porch swing or on his steps. We would usually talk for a few minutes, and then his mother would call him inside.

One day, I asked Kenny's mother if he could stay outside to talk a little longer.

She answered me in her usual demeaning manner, "No, Kenny can't just play like you boys, he has to study. Don't you know he's a child prodigy?"

As we used to say in the Air force: I got the message Five by Five. LOUD AND CLEAR!

During the summer, when school was out, I was invited into Kenny's house for short visits.

Supposedly, it was to hear Kenny recite prose or play the piano. Invariably, after only several minutes, Kenny's mother would take over the entertainment. She would happily demonstrate her talents.

At the end of her performance, his mother would always give us a plate of cookies and a glass of milk. It was our well earned reward for being her captive audience. I was thankful for the treats.

Once, after much pestering, Kenny's mother reluctantly allowed Kenny to go with me on a family outing to Lake Ponchartrain. We had a picnic and even went swimming in the pre-pollution lake. My mother says he even spent a weekend with us in Bay St. Louis, Mississippi.

My memories of these two highly unusual events are uncertain at best, but since my oldest sister has photographs, I guess they prove that those events really happened.

Thinking back on Kenny's childhood, I came to realize just how much Kenny's mother ruled his life. He wasn't just her child; he was her most valuable possession.

Kenny never resisted his mother's wishes, and he never showed any signs of anger towards her when I was around. Whenever she called him inside, a sad expression of resignation was his only outward sign of emotion. He was totally accepting of his situation. His life was the life she planned for him.

My relationship with Kenny changed after I finished grammar school. I started high school earlier than Kenny, and he later went to a different high school.

We were out of touch completely by the time we each went to different colleges.

My family moved to the other side of town the same year that I went away to college in Baton Rouge. Kenny moved away too, but I can't actually remember whether or not I moved away from the old neighborhood first, or if Kenny moved away before I did.

In truth, I totally lost contact with Kenny. I never even thought about him for years. I was busy leading my own life. I had always assumed that he would be a great success.

I knew Kenny was really very smart and talented, and his mother always told me he was a genius. She had meticulously planned his life so that someday he could make her famous as his mentor. He always did everything he was told.

After graduating from college, I went on active duty in the Air Force to become a real-life jet-jockey. After my five year commitment to the service was completed, I came back to New Orleans to resume civilian life. By then I had a wife and two daughters, so I went about the job of trying to build a civilian career.

My first job was with the American Can Company, where I worked for several years before starting a real estate management and construction business in 1965.

Several more busy years had passed by, when in 1969, I read a small newspaper article about my old boyhood friend Kenny.

The report related the grim details of Kenny's premature death.   Kenny, feeling distraught and desperate, committed suicide at 32 years of age.

My kind and gentle boyhood friend, who couldn't bear to hurt anything, took out all of his frustrations on himself. Even though I hadn't thought about Kenny in years, vivid memories of our childhood came to mind instantly.

I could easily understand his fatal depth of despair. I wondered whether Kenny had even momentarily achieved the success his mother had demanded.

Had he ever lived up to her great expectations? I wondered had he ever escaped her manipulation and domination? I wondered if Kenny had ever been happy.

No, Kenny never found his happiness. His despair was evidently so great that he must have thought his only way out of his feelings of failure was to end his seemingly useless existence. Suicide must have been a blessed relief from his sad and tormented pseudo life.

Kenny is one of life's tragedies. He lost hope. Kenny thought his life would never be any different. I understood his torment.

Most of us go through periods of deep depression and despair as a part of our natural human maturing process. Kenny suffered from a chronic case of low self-esteem, and he succumbed to an acute attack of total despair. In his mind he was a failure. He thought he could never achieve the fame and fortune his mother craved.

If you've ever experienced such a morbid feeling of desperation, you'll know exactly how he undoubtedly reasoned. In his mind, he knew the world would surely be better off without him in it.

Kenny never told me that he wanted to be known as a genius. He never really wanted to be different from the rest of us. All he ever wanted to be was a normal person. He just wanted to be happy.

After Kenny died, I realize that as a child he wasn't as lucky as I was. Nobody ever taught him that it was all right to just be himself.

Kenny simply never understood that just because his mother insisted that he was gifted with more brain power than most of us, he didn't have to prove it to the world.

In spite of his intelligence, Kenny tragically failed the final exam of life. He made the wrong and eventually fatal choice. Instead of choosing to be himself, he chose to try to be the person his mother thought he should be.

He vainly placed all of his hopes for happiness on accomplishing what she wanted him to achieve. It was she who craved the fame and fortune, not her son. Kenny's sad story didn't end there.

Even after his death, his mother never gave up her control over Kenny. She was determined to prove to the world that she had surely produced a rare genius, cloned in her image. She was pit-bull determined, and she never gave up.

Eleven years after Kenny died, she finally got her wish.

After many years of relentlessly pursuing the publication of the novel he had written before his death, it was finally published.

Her dead son, my boyhood friend named Kenny, is now, in fact, widely recognized as the literary genius who wrote the prize winning book, "A Confederacy of Dunces,"

She had finally proven that she had given birth to and molded a prodigy. She had created a genius, and the world finally had to accept it. When Kenny was posthumously awarded a Pulitzer Prize, she had finally reached her life's only real goal.

It was the crowning glory of her relentless quest for fame and fortune. Thelma Toole then became the "Queen" of the New Orleans literary court. She eagerly took her position at the center of the cultural stage. At last, she had an audience all for herself, enticed to pay her homage on the power of her dead son's talent.

I never had a desire to visit Kenny's mother during her fifteen minutes of fame. I had too many memories of his childhood, and, in truth, I was angry with her. I felt like she had not only controlled his life, she had even stolen his fame.

I'm told that after his book was awarded the Pulitzer Prize, Kenny's mother would make reporters endure sitting through one of her personal recitals before they would be rewarded with an interview. And, of course, a plate of cookies. It was the same ritual that Kenny and I had gone through so many years before. It's strange how some people never change.

Kenny had written another book titled "The Neon Bible" when he was only sixteen years old. Even though his mother had refused to let it be published while she was alive, her estate finally published it after she died.

I've read both of Kenny's books. I guess they have a special meaning to me, because I knew some of his dunces personally.

Kenny's life story had a sad beginning and a bizarre and even sadder ending. But the real tragedy of Kenny's short story is that it didn't have to happen that way.

Certainly Kenny didn't become more talented because he killed himself. Lots of people kill themselves. He didn't have to die to become talented. He always was talented. He just wasn't happy, with himself or with life.

Why was he so unhappy? That's simple. He never learned to love himself. Kenny suffered from a very negative self-image. His only life was the life that he allowed his mother to force on him.

Kenny never chose a life of his own. He had no choice as a child, but he could have made different choices when he became a man.

Kenny died a young man in the prime of his life, and his mother died an eccentric old lady. Was either a success? Certainly not in my book. I don't believe that success is a point you reach in life. Success is the way you live your journey through life.

As Dr. Robert Schuller says:

"Success is never ending, and failure is never final."

Even truly happy people experience ups and downs, but they always retain an enduring level of self-love.

All of the really successful people that I've known have all been truly happy people. As for me, I don't need to be convinced any further. I know for certain that my happiness is the only true gauge of my success. It's up to me.

If you wish to argue that everyone needs to achieve some measure of worldly success in order to be happy, then at least you'll surely allow me to at least propose that your happiness should only be judged by your own standards of success.

You can't determine what success is for others, and others shouldn't impose their ideas of success on you. We are each free to pursue our own course of happiness, as long as we don't do anything that infringes on any other person's well being.

Many people strive to achieve great wealth and fame, and some surely make it. They imagine that having lots of money will make them happy, but real success can't be measured in the worldly realm of monetary **C E N T S.**

Answer this simple question: How many times have you seen super rich and famous people who are totally miserable? Just look at some of the famous stars of Hollywood. They're miserable, and they often try to make everyone around them miserable too.

Public achievement is merely a fragile glass trophy, sitting high on a wobbly pedestal, bringing only fleeting satisfaction.

After more than thirty years of working with others, I can tell you for sure that when all else fails to bring you happiness, the **"Golden Rule"** works.

I believe that gaining wisdom is one of our primary reasons for existence, and that successfully meeting our daily challenges is the real enjoyment of life.

Real success is found in accepting who you are, and in doing what you like to do.

Success comes from the inner security of knowing that you are trying to do the best that you can do, and by being happy with your own efforts. Don't judge others, and let others seek and find their happiness in their own way.

What is success worth? How should success be judged? Real success comes by mixing equal proportions of the four senses of happiness that sustain a peaceful state of mind.

A true and lasting "Sense of Success" is formed from these four states of consciousness, which I firmly believe comprise all that is necessary to be a truly happy human being:

A Sense of Self Worth and Self Love
A Sense of Love and Respect for Others
A Sense of Security and Serenity
A Sense of Humor

The first step in maintaining personal happiness and success is:

A Sense of Self-Worth and Self-Love.

Don't just take my word on this. I'd love to take the credit, but as I've already admitted, it's not my idea. I didn't make it up. I got it from Coca Cola, and Coke got it from the Bible.

A number of years ago, a book came out titled "I'm OK, You're OK", by Thomas A. Harris. It was a best seller, and I highly recommend it. But, I submit that the real root psychology behind his book isn't anything new either. I believe that it has the same genesis as the original "Golden Rule".

It's the same formula for happiness that's been around for thousands of years. It's just another way of saying: "Love your neighbor as you love yourself." It's still as powerful as ever, because it works.

On night, I was watching Barbara Walters, the highly respected American television personality, interviewing Barbra Streisand. It was shortly before Streisand was going to be appearing in a live concert in front of a paying audience for the fist time in more than twenty years.

She told Barbara Walters that she hadn't appeared in person for all those years because she was afraid to make a mistake. She was afraid she would forget the words to her songs.

Is it hard to imagine the most successful female singer of our time being afraid to appear in person? She said she could appear in person for free, but not for money.

I understood exactly what she meant. If she appeared for free, she felt she didn't have to be perfect.

When Barbara Walters asked her about what she wanted to do with the rest of her life. She said she wanted to find out more about life, and what was missing in hers. She wanted to learn more about what it meant to "Love your neighbor....as you love yourself."

In a nutshell, this is what she wants to understand. If you love yourself, then you can love others as well. If you don't know how to love yourself, how can you know how to love me?

On the other hand, if you don't love yourself, why should I love you?

If we're in something together, how can I be successful if you're not successful?

True success starts with you loving you, and thrives on your love for others.

I can guarantee you that the formula for real happiness can truly be found in the simple yet most powerful piece of advice that Barbra Streisand said she wants to understand:

"Love your neighbor, as you love yourself."

You don't need to love others more than you love yourself, just not any less than you love yourself. The key is to loving yourself first. It's the only way you'll ever have positive and long lasting self-esteem.

The second part of the equation is:

A Sense of Respect and Love for Others.

It's the "You're Ok" part of the deal.

It's the "love your neighbor" side of success. One thing is certain; nobody achieves any degree of worldly success completely by themselves. No matter how you judge worldly success, you can't achieve it all alone.

Richard Gere, also a successful Hollywood movie star, was also interviewed by Barbara Walters during another of her television shows.

She asked Gere if it was important for him to be loved. He thought for a minute, and then answered Barbara Walters with just two words: "To love". Then he made this point: "Being loved is easy. It's easy to get people to love me. The hard thing is learning to love other people." Learning to love others is only possible when you really love yourself.

I've learned a lot about people by watching Barbara Walters. Getting to know more about people is one of my favorite pastimes.

If you're a happy person, then more than likely a happy person raised you.

A TIMELESS TIP

> **You're never too smart**
>
> **to learn something new**
> **from someone else.**

If you're happy with the talents you have, then more than likely someone with talent was secure enough in themselves to praise you. If you're happy with the work you do, then more than likely somebody is happy to pay you for doing it.

Not only is happiness success, the best way to maintain success is to encourage those around you to be just as successful as they can be. Happiness breeds happiness.

Happiness is a sense of being. It's a condition of the mind. In the spiritual realm, it's known as the state of grace. Happiness is a gift you get for free. No one needs to make you happy, and, conversely, none can make you happy.

Other people can do certain things that can trigger a negative or positive reaction in you. You can become mad, you can feel sad, or even be glad. You can laugh at other people and with other people, but no one else can make you happy.

I heard this statement during a sermon in church one Sunday: "The saddest thing I can think of is someone getting to the end of their life and not finding happiness in heaven."

I'm not preaching heresy, but I can't be a part of that waiting for the pot-of-gold philosophy of life. The saddest thing that I can think of is someone spending their whole life living through their own little hell-on-earth, trying to make sure they find happiness at the end of the rainbow.

Happiness is not the absence of problems. Happiness never demands perfection.

Happiness is definitely also not "ever having to say you're sorry." Everyone makes missstakes.

The good news and the bad news about happiness are both the same: Your happiness is totally up to you.

I wish it wasn't so, but my friend Kenny was one of life's ultimate losers. He wasn't a loser because he didn't have what it takes to win; he just didn't believe he did. He just gave up on life. You can't win when you forfeit the game.

The third step on the stairway to success is:

A Sense of Security and Serenity.

Fear of failure is the most destructive fear of all. Physical fear is a natural occurrence, and should be recognized and acted upon accordingly.

Mental security and serenity is already preprogrammed within each of us. It doesn't have to be earned. It's there for the having. We only need to learn to love ourselves, and to accept the inner peace and serenity that real self-love provides.

The whole world is full of happiness and success; all we have to do is recognize it.

20

Mark Twain wrote:

"Courage is the resistance to fear.
The mastery of fear.
It is not the absence of fear."

Having inner peace doesn't guarantee that we won't ever have to face real problems. It doesn't mean that Mother Nature won't disrupt our neat little plans. It doesn't mean that we won't ever experience sorrow, pain, and suffering. People who truly love themselves have security, serenity, and an inner peace that gives them the courage to face whatever life sends their way.

At one time, the American dream for many people was working for a big corporation until retirement. In today's competitive world, ruled by cheap foreign labor, downsizing, and bankruptcies, that once-upon-a-time fantasy has turned into a real life nightmare for many.

You must have a strong sense of security and self-confidence in order to survive in today's competitive job market.

The only real job security you have is within yourself. It's the security of knowing that you can do a good job no matter where you find work.

Effective management and being able to move successfully from one industry to another is predicated on understanding these five basic elements of knowledge, which we'll discuss more fully in a later Chapter.

Knowing what you know, when you know it.

Knowing what you don't know, when you don't know it.

Knowing what you need to know.

Knowing who knows what you need to know.

Knowing how to get them to let you know what they know.

I'm not suggesting that anyone can simply manage any company, without quickly gaining the technical knowledge needed to operate within a specific industry.

I am advocating that the basic process of managing is the same for every business.

Thousands of highly competent managers change industries every day, without any problems. Detailed technical knowledge can be learned as it is needed. Lots of people retire from one profession and start another.

Some of the very largest corporations in this country are now being lead by former military officers. That's a real change of professions!

Competent people are competent people, regardless of the type of work they do. If no one else will give you a job, give yourself a job. Open a business. The sky's the limit.

The final step for achieving your full measure of happiness is:

A Sense of Humor.

When life becomes all work and no play, it's definitely not much fun. People without a sense of humor lead dull lives. Once again, I submit that self-confidence is the key to having an active sense of humor. A good sense of humor starts when you love yourself enough to laugh at your own mistakes and your differences.

My daddy always told me that it was better to have someone laughing with you than laughing at you.

Even when someone else laughs at you, and you're laughing at yourself along with them, then at least you're both laughing at the same time.

When you have a good sense of humor, people laugh with you. When you look for the fun and enjoyment in your work, a good sense of humor usually develops naturally.

Effective managers never take life too seriously. Even when a bad thing happens, after a little time has passed, there is generally some humor found in looking at the things that went wrong. Of course, that's only true when the results of the incident weren't too tragic.

When people ask me why I sometimes laugh at times of trouble, I tell them this: "Well, you can either laugh or you can cry, and crying isn't much fun."

Certainly, every job has some aspects that are not enjoyable.

Jobs involving physical danger and high risk are, by their very nature, externally stressful jobs.

While the stress of danger can be a problem, it's usually internal stress resulting from job dissatisfaction that causes more destructive personal problems.

A TIMELESS TIP

> **If your job ceases to be fun,
> do something else.**

I believe there is a **Fun/Stress Factor** related to every kind of job. It directly affects your self-motivation and the company's morale. Have you checked out yours? A high-stress/low-fun factor will cause you trouble either at work or at home, and generally in both places.

I urge you to keep your **"Fun Factor"** way up on the high side of the fun scale. People with high levels of self-esteem function with high levels of fun in their work.

The danger point is this:

If your fun factor is not considerably greater than your personal stress factor, sooner or later you're going to have a serious personal problem.

Contrary to what you might conclude by watching daytime television dramas, (we used to call them soap operas) I find that most of the people I've known do have a fairly healthy self-image.

I guess that kind of thinking puts me in the company of the traditional **"Y"** type managers. Managers who practice positive thinking usually do have more fun.

In practice, there are many times when a good manager must combine the typical **"X"** and **"Y"** styles. Sometimes a dictator, sometimes a gentle persuader. They understand the practical approach.

Faced with relentless competition, most of our country's largest corporations have moved to a formalized quality management concept.

"Total Quality Management" is built on the idea that responsibility for the success of a company rests with each and every individual employee.

Each individual must be just as concerned about the success of every other individual working for the company. Every person counts.

Consistent leadership quality calls for managers who can seize the moment, lead people effectively, and who have a fertile imagination and vision for the future. This pragmatic style aptly describes all of the many successful entrepreneurial managers that I've known. They understand how their whole business functions. Let's call them "**E**" style managers.

I promised that this wasn't going to be a scientific essay, but I'll take literary license to advance this quasi-mathematical formula for labeling Street Smart Managers. Let's call them "**S**" style managers for short.

The following pseudo mathematical equation describes Street Smart Management:

$$(X) + (Y) + (E) = (S)$$

A positive self-image helps Street Smart Managers make the right choices that insure their happiness and success.

In the subsequent chapters we'll look at how a positive self-image will help you make the choices that will insure your happiness and success in the working world.

CHAPTER 2

"Baby Steps"

God helps those who help themselves.

People told me that sitting down to write this book wasn't going to be easy, and that just getting started would be the hardest part. They were right! It was! But I've always enjoyed a good challenge.

Like the time in when I stuck my neck way out on the old chopping block by making a risky, do-or-die proposition to the president of my company. As the local marketing manager, I made this far reaching proposal:

"Put me completely in charge of the company's perennial money losing Louisiana asphalt refining operations and we'll make a profit within a year."

I was really betting on a winner-take-al-long-shot. I even vowed that if we didn't make a profit within the year I would resign. I guess I'm one of those people that go crazy over a chance to do something challenging. Most of the people in the Texas headquarters thought that I was just plain crazy, and maybe they were right.

Everyone knew that I didn't have one day's worth of asphalt refining experience, and even though that was true, the president accepted my bold offer anyway, and he put me in charge of the whole operation.

Even with several millions of dollars of annual sales, the refinery had recorded many thousands of dollars in losses in each of the previous ten years. Reversing an unbroken record of ten straight losing years was the job I took on. I wasn't worried about taking over. I was still fairly young, and I figured that I could always dig ditches for a living if I had to.

I guess I was overly confident, but without realizing it at the time, I inherently understood the two steps for guaranteed success. I had faith in myself, and I had great faith in the other people who were going to be working with me. All I had to do was help them be successful.

I knew that all of the local employees were already working hard. They just weren't working smart. I knew that if the plant supervisors were just given enough support, they would get the best from the people working under them. I had no doubt that, when everybody knew that everybody counted, we were going to be successful. Initially, I faced a crucial and very critical task. Training!

Neither the refinery manager, nor any of the supervisors working under him, had ever received any type of training. All of the plant supervisors had been promoted from the ranks.

I still have the original outline of the first supervisor training program that I had hurriedly put together. It was handwritten on a yellow legal pad. I didn't have time to make it fancy and formal. We just had to get to work.

Happily, the training worked very well, and our people excelled beyond all of the expectations of the corporate headquarters. Of course, all along I had expected that we would all be highly successful.

Failure wasn't in my vocabulary. Maybe I just didn't know any better. We all just went along, fat, dumb, and happy; doing lots of things we were having fun doing. It worked!

To paraphrase from the popular country and western song, **"We were Quality, before Quality was cool."** We started making a steady net profit well before the end of that first year.

We were happy, and justly proud of what we had accomplished, and as a result of it, we were well rewarded. To us, the important point was that we didn't wait to enjoy the public recognition that came from reaching our goal; we had fun during the entire process.

It was great fun, and everybody was happy. Needless to say, I didn't have to dig ditches, and I didn't resign. I even stayed around a few more years, until I got another job offer that I just couldn't refuse.

Realistically, I've faced the problem of inadequate management preparation in each and every organization that I've worked with over the past thirty years.

I've conducted nearly two hundred personal opinion surveys during my various management training seminars. According to those numerous surveys, things haven't really changed very much in management and leadership training over the last two decades.

Poor supervisory effectiveness, resulting from a lack of management training, remains one of the most serious problems facing most industries today.

In answers to research survey questions about where they saw their company's biggest problems, one hundred and ninety (190) respondents, from sixty-nine (69) different private companies, government agencies, and non-profit organizations listed poor employee training as the main problem they faced in their daily operations.

Training related problems were brought out by ninety-four percent (94%) of the food and hospitality managers involved in this research.

This poor training phenomenon is easily understood when you stop to think that there has been very little opportunity for people to find practical supervisory training courses through our old-line high schools and colleges. More often than not, most supervisory training, if any, is informal; and strictly on-the-job.

According to these research findings, difficulties with employee attitudes and problems with poor employee motivation come in closely behind poor training. These kinds of concerns were brought out by eighty-eight percent (88%) of the respondents.

Three other management problems were also mentioned as needing special attention: 1) Conflict and stress on the job, 2) Poor communications, and 3) Meeting competition.

Should these statistics concern you? They concern me! To help bring my point home, it's important to look at what makes this information valid and worthwhile.

This down-to-earth, candid evaluation of management's problems isn't just a bunch of useless facts and figures that were gathered up for some academic exercise.

All of the participants in this on going management research project were real working people, just like you and me. They face the same kinds of things you face in your work every day. Because they too wanted to be more successful, they agreed to take a close look at their own management experiences within their real-life situations.

This ongoing seven year study represents a wide array of management experience, in the number of years in management, the number of people supervised, and the level of responsibility. The study group was composed of senior, mid-level, and front-line managers. It included supervisors engaged in many types of large and small businesses.

Most of these managers were originally promoted to supervisory positions directly from the ranks of operational workers. Several of them had some managerial experience before they were hired for their present positions, but only a few had ever had formal management training.

Many companies are started by a person, with a marketable trade or skill, who bravely decides to become self-employed. They either want to make more money or just be their own boss. Many of these people go into business totally untrained for the job of management.

As these rudimentary management research statistics mentioned above show, when a supervisory opening occurs, many companies routinely promote the most skilled technician or the most productive person in the department to the new position.

However, technical skill alone does not prepare someone for the job of managing others and the ability to manage people is the primary key to all lasting success in the working world.

Most ambitious people sooner or later find themselves faced with supervising others at some point in their careers. This is the typical way that most people get ahead in business.

Millions and millions of people are traveling along the same rocky road toward the Emerald City. They place getting rich as their ultimate goal.

Meanwhile, back in the real world, only a very limited few ever hit the jackpot. That's why it's so very important for the rest of us to understand what being a successful manager is truly all about.

As you'll discover later, my fundamental recipe for success is not something new. I wish I could take the credit for it, but it's not something I dreamed up. What's more, the really good news is that it works for everybody that believes and understands it.

Unfortunately, many of the management books that I've read present the role of a supervisor simply as a bit player in a technically oriented, scientifically controlled, management theater, where everyone's on stage. Countless books and articles have been written extolling the virtues of various techno-fad theories and mechanical management systems.

Some espouse a robot approach to managing people, based on meeting rigid schedules, making set quotas, and constantly reducing the cost of labor.

I wanted this book to be different. This is a book written for and about ordinary people. I wanted this book to be easy to read, easy to understand, easy to remember, and very easy to put into practice.

I wanted it to be a handy little book that you could put down and pick up again without having to remember a bunch of technical stuff from the previous chapters. I wanted to pass on some of the down-to-earth, real-world, practical knowledge, and experience that I've gathered over a life time of facing life in the fascinating world of business, one day at a time.

When I started thinking about what I should write about, I asked myself these three questions:

Is there one thing about management that is so basic that it affects every worker, every line supervisor, every middle manager, and every senior executive in every organization?

Is there any important thing that I've learned concerning success?

Is there actually a formula for successful management?

In my mind, the answer to all of these questions is a definite, enthusiastic, exciting, and totally satisfying yes!

The best part is that the concept of true success is so very simple.

Looking back over the last sixty years, I realize that I had already learned the most important thing about real success by the time I had reached the age of reason. By the time I was seven years old, I already understood that everyone has certain basic needs and wants.

When I was hungry, I needed to eat. When I was thirsty, I needed to drink. When I was sleepy, I needed to sleep. When I was in danger, I needed security. When it was raining, I needed a place to stay dry and warm. When I needed to know something, I needed to ask someone who knew it, or I needed to read a book so I could learn something about it. When I was alone and lonely, I wanted companionship. When I did something good, I wanted praise. When I did something wrong, I wanted to be forgiven. I knew that grown-ups had to work. I knew my family loved me just because I was me, and that being loved felt good.

I was even learning to understand what he meant when Daddy often told me:

"God helps those who help themselves."

All of these things still make perfect sense, and just like everyone else, I still have every one of these same needs.

Let me quickly admit that reaching the age of reason and being reasonable are two totally different concepts.

I'm sure you know a few people that aren't ever reasonable. In reality, we live in a world populated with difficult and unreasonable people.

It's true that it takes all kinds to make a world, and most of us don't have the luxury of only associating with reasonable people. Have you ever heard of a business that didn't serve people? Serving people is the constant challenge of management. Pretty simple stuff, right?

Basic, yes! Simple, No! The immutable truth of the matter is that every single person on earth is affected by the same basic needs and wants in more or less the same way.

People are people, no matter what kind of work they do, and the people that you work with are basically no different than most other people. People are the same, but each person is unique.

The priorities that people place on their various needs and wants change drastically from person to person, usually depending on their economic status.

Overall, the priorities people seem to place on their needs and wants become less uniform as their income increases beyond the poverty level.

I'm sure that some learned anthropologist or sociologist would have more intellectual and comprehensive explanations of the differences between needs and wants.

In the United States in particular, it seems that managers must deal more often with trying to understand and satisfy their employees' higher ego needs rather than meeting their basic needs.

For my purposes, I place people's "needs" in the area of their physical requirements, and I classify people's "wants" in a category of ego satisfaction.

People's egos generally come into real play only after they have met their fundamental needs for survival and security. The truth is: Most American workers easily meet their basic physical needs.

Beyond the basic needs, everyone has the same general ego serving wants and desires. All people want to be happy, feel worthwhile, be appreciated, be loved, and have someone that they can love. It's the method they choose to meet these wants and desires that differs from person to person.

Did you ever notice that great wealth usually doesn't turn out to be one of the things that make people happy after they get it? In short, meeting ego fulfilling wants and desires is not what success is all about.

It's not about just making a lot of money. Money alone cannot satisfy these basic ego requirements.

So much severely depressing unhappiness is caused by confusing the need for achieving true personal satisfaction with attaining worldly success.

Generally this form of major mental misery is a greater problem in affluent societies, where "What you are" receives more attention than "Who you are."

What you do to make money can change in a split second. But, thank God, **you are who you are** for a lifetime. No person and nothing can change who you are, unless you let them.

If you're reading this book, it's probably because you initially thought that I would tell you how to become financially secure. That's exactly what I plan to do.

What's more, I can tell you that you don't have to wait to be promoted, or to have a bunch of money in the bank in order to feel financially secure.

As I promised in the title, you only have to be ready to take two small steps to get on the winning track. If you follow these two steps faithfully, your life will never be the same.

If you're finding that you're not really having much fun in your personal life or with your work, these two steps will profoundly change your life for the better.

Serenity will be both instant and constant. You'll learn to understand that it's not money that produces financial security. However, before you can take those two steps you must become a true believer. You need to fully understand just how simple, yet powerful, these two life affirming actions are.

When people place all of their hopes for happiness in achieving riches and egocentric worldly successes, they usually have serious problems dealing with the excesses that result from their successes.

Alcohol, drugs, depression, violence, and suicide are all too commonly found among people who have never learned that true success can only come from within. True success is totally under your control. Each one of us owns the deed to our own castle of success, and no one can take it away unless you let them.

Why do so many people who hit the top end up on the bottom? Why do many of them take their own lives? Because, happiness seldom follows from worldly success. Happiness is only enhanced by wordily success. Normally, people aren't any happier after they get rich than they were before they got rich.

Money and power don't bring happiness. But, on the other hand, happy people usually remain happy even when they have money and power. In fact, happiness and taking joy from your work usually precedes and breeds financial success.

Truly successful people don't base all of their happiness on what they do, and certainly not on what they have accomplished. Fame is often for just a fleeting moment in time. Then it just becomes a fading memory.

When it comes to true success, it matters very little what someone has achieved. What really matters is how happy a person is. The way they feel inside, and how they live their life. Truly successful people rely on themselves first, and they place a strong faith in others.

Of course, we all do have to eat, so let's not forget the practical problem of making enough money to meet your needs. The best route to long term financial success in a free enterprise economy is through productivity.

No matter what job you have and no matter what kind of work you perform, you'll be more effective and reach higher goals when you are satisfied with your efforts.

In my experience, I've always found that happy people are the most productive people. I've also found that many unhappy people tend to want everybody else to be unhappy along with them. Misery sure does love company.

I think the word happy describes a person who has already taken the first step to success. Unhappy describes a person who doesn't even understand the meaning of step number one.

Employee discontent is one of the biggest problems facing management today. Human resource practitioners have all kinds of fancy names for this common malady, but in the end it's still just plain old unhappiness.

One day, an associate and I were having a talk about some of my early career management troubleshooting experiences, and she wanted to know if I thought management problems have changed over the years. She asked me this question: "Do I look for different kinds of problems now than I did thirty years ago?"

I answered: "No. I don't really approach things any differently now. Most management problems today are the same as they have always been.

Time and time again, I've found that most employee problems stem from some trouble deep-seated within a really unhappy person. But, I do think that after all these years, I have definitely gained more wisdom for dealing with those problems."

I have attempted to pass on some of that wisdom in this book, and make it a book that's useful for everyday situations. It's not a typical management textbook. It contains no complicated statistics or complicated theoretical concepts. This is not a technical book.

In fact, **(X) + (Y) + (E) = (S)** is the only formula you'll find in this book

Think of this book as a "Primer" for success. It's for all of those special people who are faced with the daily task of supervising others, whether by fancy or by fate.

These concepts, which I group under the title of Street **Smart Management**, are based on my own interpretation of actual circumstances and real situations that I've personally experienced in my management career.

I've been a fascinated observer of the many ordinary and successful people I've known. This book is about real things that happen to real people, in real businesses, time and time again.

Whether you want to use the word leader, manager, or supervisor; my working definition is identical for each one of these common titles. I describe each one as a person who has to work closely with and serve other people.

Managers are just normal people, who have taken on the responsibility for helping others do the things that have to be done.

This book is essentially devoted to the human aspects of achieving business success through managerial leadership.

Whether you work with only one other person, or whether you supervise large departments full of people, these same hands-on concepts are valid in all cases. These winning ways work for people in all walks of life.

Street Smart Management is not the latest fad in an endless list of what is loosely termed scientific management theories. It's definitely not a complicated and systematic robotic method for managing a business. Managing people successfully is definitely not scientific or mechanical. Street Smart Management is an approach to supervision that cannot be easily divided into discrete little pieces. The concept is more an attitude towards management than a check list of things to do.

My focus points are two fundamental and essential steps that will get you started on the winning track to success. You'll win through excellence, excitement, enthusiasm, and enjoyment.

A TIMELESS TIP

> **A chain is only as strong
> as its weakest link.**

When each manager becomes as successful as possible, the company chain will be strong enough to pull the load.

Miss out on the strength of one person on the team, and the chain falls apart.

The good news is that there is nothing mystical or magical about being a successful business manager. You only need to understand and practice the few sound fundamentals of Street Smart Management that will be presented. These same people oriented management methods have produced positive results for thousands of years, and I have absolutely no doubt that they will continue to do so forever.

Street Smart Management is the human approach to enjoying true success in business management.

In the following chapters, we'll talk about authority and full responsibility, true self-esteem, self-motivation, good communications, planning and problem solving, empowerment, and teamwork.

CHAPTER 3

"In Control"

> **Leadership is simply taking the responsibility for helping others get the job done.**

"**FOLLOW ME**"! For more than five years of my life, I eagerly looked forward to seeing those two authoritative words appear in front of my eyes, especially at night, on a strange military air field.

Those reassuring words were displayed on a large sign on the back of a truck. It was the truck that would lead my air ship to a safe berth on the parking ramp.

Seeing that familiar sign meant that I had once again cheated death. I knew that after another long and tedious mission, I had made it safely back to good old terra firma. And once again, I had escaped the dubious thrill of an unwanted parachute jump.

I still can't understand why any sane person would voluntarily jump out of a perfectly good airplane. They even call it fun.

The driver of the truck was usually a low ranking airman. As a pilot, I was an officer and usually in charge, but, for that moment on the field, he was my leader. He controlled me. He led the way and I gladly followed. I needed his service, and he fulfilled the important function of leadership while he provided it.

Driving a "Follow Me" truck is a job that requires intelligence, physical ability, and great responsibility. Military planes don't come cheap.

Even in the military, leadership is never completely defined simply by the chain of command or a rigid set of rules and regulations. Leadership is never defined by the official position that a person holds. Leadership is earned respect.

A TIMELESS TIP

> **Managers who can't inspire,
> will soon expire.**

Leadership is the ability to make things happen. Working for the service and benefit of others marks the identity of a true leader. Meeting people's needs and wants is what real leadership is all about.

In the business world, the tendency is to think of the leaders of a company as those people in various management positions with their names on the organizational chart.

Generally, that's a fairly safe assumption, but there's a lot more that goes into effective management than just being placed on the company's official roster.

Having a position listed on the company organizational chart usually denotes a position of power, but understanding how to use that power effectively is what makes a Street Smart Manager successful.

Webster's Seventh New Collegiate Dictionary defines **"Power"** as: **"Possession of control, authority, or influence over others."**

"Control" is described as: **direction, regulation, coordination of production, administration, and other business activities.**

"Authority" is explained as: **"persons in command"**, and in the descriptive narrative of **"Influence"** it states that it: **"may apply to a force exercised and received unknowingly or to a conscious and deliberate affecting."**

In every sense a business manager is a person with power. A manager is a person who controls and influences others, simply because he or she has the power to do so. In this chapter we will look at how authority is achieved, maintained, and often lost; and we'll start to investigate the leadership style of the Street Smart Manager.

In order to understand the leadership role of a modern business manager, we need to look at the basic characteristics and functions of leadership; and discuss the evolution of management styles. We need to study the changes over time.

Here's a brief look at how I envision the role of leadership and how it has changed over the history of our civilization.

The first leaders controlled others by physical power alone. Currently, leaders more often than ever exercise control primarily through their influence over others. That's the difference.

If you want different viewpoints on the evolution of leadership, I'm sure there are many anthropologists, biologist, sociologist, and other "ologist" who will enthusiastically give you their opinions.

My practical assessment of the developments in leadership is not necessarily based on hard scientific facts, and it contains no historical names and dates. But it works for me. Of course, none of us has been there through it all. So who's to say I'm not pretty close to right.

Truthfully, the only thing that really matters is to have a general understanding of the changes that have occurred, and to seek to understand what those changes mean for us today.

Long before the advent of private businesses of any kind, the first leaders were probably the head male in a single family. The first families probably lived in caves, in single family units by themselves. The leader was the person who brought in the food and kept predators away.

These early families were only concerned with their basic needs: food, water, shelter, and safety. Everybody was in the same economic fix. Everybody lived day-to-day.

As family units grew in number, I think they probably started living in groups because it was easier to hunt and forage together. They could share the work and the food. Humans still have the tendency to do things the easy way.

As more groups started expanding into each other's territory, protection of the tribe's own land became important. Tribal chiefs came along to help keep rival tribes from stealing their goods, stealing the women, and killing all of the male members of their tribe.

Stronger tribes found that it was easier to steal a weaker tribe's food than to hunt for themselves. This is what hyenas and lions do to other lesser predators. Humans, at the top of the predatory chain, often show signs of the same behavior.

No doubt the road to leadership during our earliest history was through brute strength. Basic survival of the fittest. This was the earliest form of assumed leadership. If you were the strongest, you assumed the position of leader.

Exactly when leaders started using gods in their efforts to control their people is unknown. It was probably when the first tribal leader realized that the people's fear of the unknown was more powerful than their fear of a mere mortal.

In any event, the earliest records of human history show that various tribes worshipped many different gods. People believed that these gods were powerful and capable of killing anyone that did not follow their wishes.

It seems only natural that tribal leaders would claim that the gods had chosen them to rule.

The number of tribes grew, and as tribes started to kill more game and harvest more crops than they needed for themselves, early signs of cross-cultural civilization emerged.

I believe this era of history marked the time when people started finding out that once they were safe and sheltered, with abundant water and food, they now wanted additional things in life. Trade between groups was a method of getting some of the things you wanted from other people that had them in surplus, without going to war.

Hunting tribes could trade meat and fur to farming tribes. Within many tribes, people who controlled the material goods were separated into two broad groups: 1) People who owned things, the (haves) and 2) Those who didn't, the (have- nots).

As tribes bonded together into loosely associated trading groups, overlords came about. I'd venture to say that the strongest chief, from the strongest tribe, became the Big Chief. He probably even claimed to be anointed by a god.

As time went on, more and more people began living in permanent places. The barter system was eventually replaced by trade for legal tender.

The process of assuming power by brute force was gradually being replaced with a more orderly method of achieving the leadership of the people. The earliest leaders strictly provided control and protection.

Maintaining stability in leadership became necessary in order to insure continuity of law and order among the people. The many gods of old tribes were gradually being replaced by the modern concept of one Supreme God.

Fast forwarding ahead, we find that kings and queens came about when amassing vast amounts of land became the best means of controlling crops, forest animals, valuable minerals, and water.

Power changed form drastically. It went from being a case of the strongest individual taking on all comers, by the strength of his power alone; to having the power to take on all comers based on the combined strength of the whole community.

Military might was used to protect royal lands and holdings, to exercise control over the ever increasing population, and to collect the taxes.

The royal leaders controlled the military by providing the soldiers with a little more material goods than they allowed the ordinary peasants to have.

Since leaders no longer needed to rely on their own brute strength, leadership could now be perpetuated simply by maintaining control of the land and the resources. Controlling the land and the resources gave a leader control over the people.

Inherited royalty became the best manner of directly passing on power and maintaining permanent control of the land, resources, and people. The royals all claimed that God gave them their authority to rule.

Kings and queens were anointed and they appointed all of the lesser people in authority. In either case, the common ordinary person still had little or no say in the selection of the leaders.

The people in power were busy satisfying their every want, while the growing masses of peasants were still barely able to meet their basic needs.

The emergence of rich merchant rulers started to change the balance of power. When the merchant rulers came into prominence, it was still a system in which a relatively few people firmly controlled the great mass of goods and people.

Society was still pretty much divided between two main groups: 1) The ruling class, and 2) Everybody else.

Kings, queens, and merchants were not only able to meet their needs, they were also lavishly attending to their own ego driven wants; while most everybody else was still barely meeting their basic needs.

The distance between the haves and the have-nots widened, and the role of one supreme God, viewed as the source of all individual rights and of all law and order in the land, became more and more prevalent as civilization progressed.

Large divisions of people worshipped a supreme God by different names, but the idea of a single, just, and merciful creator became the true foundation for the basic human rights for all of the ordinary people in the Western World. The American Revolution forever changed everything.

The have-nots finally decided they had had enough. A new form of government was formed that proclaimed a unique theory, which simply stated that everyone has the same God given rights. Not just the leaders, and not just the rich and powerful. It directly leads to our current free enterprise system, under which most of the western world lives today.

Democracy and capitalism changed the world forever.

Under the free enterprise system, the law of supply and demand is the main force which allows the general population to pursue more and more of their needs and wants.

Revolutions have taken place throughout history, and it sure looks like they'll probably continue forever. In 1917, when the Russian have-nots decided they wanted more, they replaced royalty with communism.

Under true communism, the state replaced God. Individuals have no rights. Only the state has rights, and the state is supposed to take care of everybody. It all sounds good on paper, but we know it doesn't work out that way.

Under communism there were still two classes: The party and the poor. The only difference after communism takes control is that the poor becomes even poorer.

Some leaders still use their power primarily for their own individual enrichment. Other leaders use their power for providing for the needs and wants of many.

The three main methods of achieving leadership have gone through a steady and natural progression. Assumed, anointed, and elected leadership are all alive and well, and are all still operative today.

In the business world, leadership is also still achieved through one or more of the same basic methods that have been in existence throughout history.

When a person decides to start their own business, they assume the role of leader. When an employee is hired or promoted to a management job, they are appointed to a position of leadership. Corporate officers and directors are elected.

The real function of business leadership is still to control; through direction, regulation, and coordination.

Admittedly, this brief exposition is not a scholarly masterpiece, but that's not what's important. What is important is to realize that not only are the various means of getting your name on the organizational chart still as active as ever, and the functions of leadership are still the same as they've been throughout our history. Now, an irreversible change has taken place in leadership styles.

Styles of leadership have changed, from the savage exercise of raw power to the use of influence as the main means of getting things done. I believe this change in leadership style is a natural outgrowth of society's constant and increasing demand for meeting more needs and wants, of more and more people.

In the final analysis, today's global economic competition is the current driving force behind continuing changes in all forms of leadership throughout the world. World wide economic competition affects all forms of leadership: Business, Political, Military, Social, and Religious.

So what does all of this mean to you as an individual business owner or manager? It means that throughout history, all successful leaders have had to face challenges and constantly adapt in order make things work. They had to be Street Smart.

History teaches us a simple basic truth about leadership: Although the world has gone through all of these changes, the authority for leadership, the functions of leadership, and the styles of leadership are all still affected by the same original elements of humanity. Leaders must meet the people's needs and wants.

It also teaches that the vast majority of people living in the world still believe that God is the ultimate source of all human rights, and that all men and women are created equal.

Even in the United States, the most powerful country in the world, we are still very much affected by the vast difference between meeting a person's basic needs and trying to satisfy their every want and desire. There's still a huge difference between the haves and the have-nots of the world.

I don't care how small or how large your company is, in some way or another, these few elemental facts will affect your every action.

How do Street Smart Managers deal with these crucial facts of life? They understand that in a business setting, the only time everybody prospers is when the whole business prospers. They also understand that while a manager certainly does have to exercise certain powers to control others, the primary role of a business manager is to provide service.

Leadership is simply the taking the responsibility for helping others to get the job done.

The basic relationship between authority and responsibility is the next very important factor that we need to discuss concerning management.

Authority and responsibility always go hand in hand. They are inseparable. You can't have one without the other.

Everything in life involves taking a risk, and if you're going to take control, you have to take the risks that go along with the control.

Lots of managers like to boast about their authority. They try to impress others with how important they are, by displaying a desk sign stating: "The Buck Stops Here."

Regrettably, what usually happens is that they stop the buck, but everybody else pays the price for their failure.

When failure follows from poor leadership, being willing to accept the full blame for the failure means absolutely nothing when the damage is done.

Avoiding failure by shouldering the responsibility for doing the job successfully to begin with is the only true barometer of effective leadership.

Management responsibility requires due diligence in every single activity, and the more authority you have, the more responsibility you must accept.

On the other hand, the opposite is just as critical. Managers at all levels must be given commensurate authority for carrying out their responsibilities. Having responsibility without authority doesn't work either.

If the driver of the "Follow Me" truck didn't have the authority to control my movements on the ground, then he couldn't be held responsible for guiding me to the proper parking space.

According to the New York Times of March 31, 1981, Alexander Haig, then the United States Secretary of State, created quite a political controversy on the day that former President Ronald Reagan was shot.

Haig's troubles started when he announced on television: "As of now, I am in control here in the White House." Many people thought he meant he was taking over as president of the country.

Was Alexander Haig saying that he had disregarded the Constitution by taking authority away from the wounded President of the United States? What about the Vice President? What about the Speaker of the House?

No. Although his choice of words may have been poor, Alexander Haig was only fulfilling what he thought was his job. He simply meant to say that, in spite of the tragic attempt on President Reagan's life, everything that he was responsible for at the White House was still under control. In other words, the Executive Branch of the government of the country was still functioning.

At that moment in time Alexander Haig fully understood his function as the leading person physically at the White House, and he was trying to tell the country that there was no need for the citizens to panic.

History records that while his public statement may have been ill advised, the truth of the test was that there was no crises in our government because of the assassination attempt.

Haig kept his position of authority and his responsibility to his country in balance. Regardless of any of the political implications in this particular case, someone must always be in charge at all times, and that's the real meaning of **"In Control,"** the title of this chapter.

**Leaders must maintain effective control
at all times.**

In the next chapter, we'll look more closely at why providing service is an essential ingredient for finding happiness and success.

CHAPTER 4

"Can I Help"

> **It's better to give than to receive**

Successful managers look upon themselves as facilitators, catalysts, and servants. They serve the customers, the workers, other managers, the stockholders, and the society. By doing so, they fundamentally serve themselves and their families. Everything we do for others, we do for ourselves. That's the magic of it.

Service to your company takes many forms. One of the most important ways a Street Smart Manager serves his or her company isn't even at the job. It's when they're doing a little bit extra on their own, selling the company to the community.

While this isn't a book about selling techniques, I believe that every manager must totally, completely, fully, and unequivocally, understand this most basic of all facts: No company can exist without sales. If I could think of any stronger words to describe how important it is to understand this undeniable fact, I would use every one of them.

People like doing business with companies that they trust. A solid reputation for trust and respect is only earned over time.

Building a positive reputation takes a lot of time and very hard work, but a hard earned good name can be totally destroyed quickly and easily.

People who talk badly and openly about their own companies are hurting themselves as much as their companies.

A TIMELESS TIP

> **Never wash a company's**
> **dirty linen in public.**
> **Just help clean it up!**

Everyone, I repeat, everyone in a company must be concerned about sales. There is no business in the world that does not need sales in order to exist. Whether it makes a product or provides a service, sales keep the company operating.

Even charitable organizations must provide some services to somebody, or they have no reason to exist. Spreading goodwill in the community is an important part of a manager's service to the company.

The story of my two friends (Sid and Mary) is worth reading for the two clear examples it provides about building a good reputation and providing community service: One good! One bad!

I met Sid and Mary during the six years that I was truly privileged to work as a volunteer technical advisor for the "Christmas in October" program in the city of New Orleans.

First, I have to say Sid and Mary shared a great love, even though they weren't married. Well actually, they were married, just not to each other.

Each year "Christmas in October" repaired and painted a growing number of houses for low-income, elderly, and disabled people. They organized over three thousand volunteers from more than fifty corporations.

In New Orleans they did this work on two weekends in October. In other places in the country this program usually takes place in April, and they call it "Christmas in April."

As a volunteer Technical Adviser to the various corporations that sponsored the work, my job was to help train and inspire the many volunteers who came to repair and paint the houses.

Sid and Mary worked for one of the world's largest oil companies, and for five years I had the great pleasure of working with them on their "Christmas in October" projects.

Sid and Mary were always at the center of their company's effort. They recruited the company volunteers. They met with the owners of the houses to plan the jobs. They organized the work crews for each weekend. They scraped, painted, nailed, cleaned, and stayed at each one of the jobs until the last volunteer left.

In the five years that I worked with them, their company completely painted and made extensive repairs to seven houses, all of which were located in low-income, distressed areas of the city of New Orleans.

Each year Sid and Mary recruited about seventy-five male and female volunteers. These good people did all of the work on their own time, for no pay. Sid and Mary were not up and coming young employees. They already held important top management jobs in the company.

Sid and Mary got no extra financial reward for what they did, and both of them gave their time and efforts to other charities also. They got no personal publicity for what they did, and they certainly didn't know I was going to write anything about them in this book.

They did what they did because they understood the concept of giving service, and they loved helping people.

Public recognition wasn't important to them, but their work ethic certainly says a lot about the kind of people they are. They set a great example for the people they worked with, and because of their efforts their company gained a tremendous amount of good will in the community.

A TIMELESS TIP

> **The best way to teach**
>
> **is to practice what you preach.**

Sid and Mary certainly offer us a great example. Now let's look at another example. One day I was discussing "Christmas in October" with the Human Resources Director of another large, well known, national corporation.

In fairness, I must say that it was a company that did not participate in the "Christmas" volunteer program.

When I told this person about working with the "Christmas in October" volunteers, he asked me: "Who pays all of you to do this?" I told him: "Nobody pays any of us."

Then he said: "Well you must get something out of it somehow." I wondered if he knew what the word volunteer meant. I guess since he obviously wouldn't think of giving up any of his free time, it was too hard for him to believe that anybody else would either.

What a sad example for a human resources director. I won't mention the name of the major corporation that he works for, but if his comments are an indication of the whole corporate social mentality, I believe they're in for some serious trouble.

In truth, we actually do get something good out of helping others. When you're strong enough to freely give help to others who are less fortunate than you, you're the one who actually benefits the most.

You get a strong feeling of fulfillment. You get a rush of happiness that's hard to describe. No wonder it's better to give than to receive. You get to look in the mirror and feel pretty good about yourself. It's a natural high that can't be duplicated with drugs or alcohol.

Mr. Joseph Ammann was confined to his home most of the time. He had had a stroke and he lived by himself. His only living family member was a devoted niece who visited him every day to fix his meals. His only possession was the home he had lived in for over sixty years, and his only income was his meager social security.

Before the volunteer crew repaired his house, the roof was leaking, the ceilings were falling in, the paint was peeling from the walls, the front porch was rotting away; and the entire house needed painting.

The house was far beyond his means to fix it, but happy and loving volunteers repaired it all. They did many thousands of dollars worth of work, free of charge. Mr. Ammann was 86 years old at the time his house was repaired and painted, and he was thrilled.

The words in this letter to Sid and Mary from Joseph Ammann's heart tell of his feelings better than I could ever hope to.

It's a letter full of deep appreciation and true brotherly love. The following words were copied directly from Mr. Ammann's hand written letter:

———————

"To my most of all, dear and Devoted Friends, Angels, yes Angels from Heaven. The most appropriate name that I can think of at this time. Angels from heaven. This is imminent, We all have to face our Creator at Death or by death.

This Christmas in October. My 86 years upon this earth, was by far, was the most and Best, Joyous celebration, I have ever experienced.

Which will be cherished by me Joseph Ammann forever. Repairing and painting my house, was a beautiful piece of workmanship. My undying gratification, Immortal and Perpetual love coming from the things that I enjoyed the most of all were the people.

Angels from heaven, who made all of this work possible. I thank each and every one of you. You a memory which is highly and very appreciative by me Ammann. Thank all of you again and again.

Therefore! I am not selfish. I am asking God for a special blessing for Mr. Sid and Mrs. Mary. For that blessing which you both so very honestly deserve. For the help you have given me from the very beginning.

When these worldly shadows come to an end, may we all share and rejoice in His promise of an everlasting Glorious reign in the Heavens above.

May these worldly shadows be surpassed by the heavenly shadows lasting through eternity, or better expressed forever. Ammann.

Till we meet again my very best of all wishes, my very and I do mean my best regards.

Joseph Ammann "Ammann" God Bless.

Since Mr. Ammann was confined to his home, he would never ever buy another quart of oil or gallon of gasoline from the oil company that employed the workers who fixed his home. But that's not why the volunteers devoted their valuable time to repairing his home. They did it because they loved themselves enough to know how good it feels when you serve others.

I've talked at length about the importance of being of service, because I firmly believe that providing service is the cornerstone and underlying function of management.

On the self enrichment side of personal development, volunteering is an excellent way to get noticed, and a great deal of leadership is assumed by simply volunteering to fill the void.

Street Smart Managers don't toot their own horns. They don't brag about how important they are. They just do their jobs. Successful leaders simply say:

"We are merely servants."

At this point, it's important to make a distinction between official titles and functional leadership.

This difference can be easily demonstrated by the old television example of how an army squadron operates: The

64

squadron commander has the title, but a Sergeant Bilko runs the squadron.

This true-to-life example might seem to over simplify this phenomenon, but it's clearly descriptive of so many unofficial leadership situations, that commonly occur in the business world. Title alone, does not a leader make. In almost every business organization, regardless of the size, there is functional leadership and influence at work. Small groups of peers usually turn to one person in their group for leadership.

Managers on the same control level generally follow the lead of one of their fellow managers. Even upper-level managers will often select a certain individual on a lower level as their confidant, and look to them as a valuable source of informal information.

Functional leaders are the real leaders in a company. Some of their names may or may not actually be listed on the organizational chart. Functional leadership seldom fully follows the official chain of command.

Street Smart Managers understand this fact of organizational life perfectly, and they use this kind of functional influence effectively.

Now that I've discussed some aspects of the leadership function, I'll concentrate on leadership style. Or more to the point, I'll explain the pragmatic style of Street Smart Managers.

Down and dirty, here's the straight skinny on developing an effective management style:

Street Smart Managers create their own style.

They know that the only thing you need to do to be successful is to simply be yourself, and do your best with what you have.

No two people and no two companies are alike. Every individual is unique, and every set of circumstances is different.

Each manager must find their own style of dealing with their own situations. The bottom line is this:

Develop a style that works for you.

Don't be disappointed that I can't give you a fast and easy definition of the Street Smart Management style. Sing out! Rejoice! You are totally free to be you.

Isn't it great that you don't have to be what someone else wants you to be? That's the greatest news of all. Of course, there are some basic (do)s and (don't)s of effective leadership, and we'll talk about some of them as we go along. We'll look at some practical things that will help you find the style that works for you.

We'll also examine some very common managerial behavior traits that normally produce similar effects on most people, both positive and negative. We'll see that there are certain management behavior patterns that can definitely cause problems with most employees.

As we continue through the book, you'll be offered numerous suggestions for management methods that usually work in normal situations.

I can't emphasize too strongly that truly effective Street Smart Managers all have certain things in common.

The "Big Three" commonalties of truly successful supervisors are these: Common goals, common sense, and common courtesy. It's my theory of "Common Commitment."

It sounds so simple. It ought not be so easy, but it is. The big problem is that some people don't know what having a common commitment means.

Good leaders meet common goals.

Good leaders use common sense.

Good leaders give common courtesy.

Several years ago, my wife called the claims office of our group medical insurance carrier to discuss a problem we were having with the payment of a claim.

She had already paid the doctor, and the insurance company had sent their claim payment check directly to our doctor in error.

My wife had included a copy of the paid doctor bill with her original claim, and had not approved direct payment to the doctor.

The claim representative explained that they had paid the doctor directly because the doctor had sent his medical report directly to the insurance company. They didn't check the form to see if the direct payment waiver had been signed by my wife.

My wife explained to the claims clerk that, since the doctor's bill was marked paid, it seemed as though common sense alone would tell them the claim payment check should have been made out to my wife instead of paying the doctor twice.

At that point, the insurance company's employee gave this curt reply: "Well, we don't use common sense." She was surely right.

A TIMELESS TIP

> **Excuses don't count.**
> **Simply say you're sorry.**

The claim clerk surely didn't meet the common goal of the company, which was to provide good service to its policy holders; and she certainly didn't give my wife the common courtesy of an honest apology on behalf of the company.

Undeniably, it's true, lots of people don't use common sense, and they don't see the necessity of a common commitment.

The last thing that we'll talk about in this chapter is how the privilege of leadership can be taken away, or as happens more often, simply given away.

If I were as talented as Elizabeth Barrett Browning, I might start by saying: "Let me count the ways." Or, maybe I could write a parody to Paul Simon's famous song. I could call it: "Fifty Ways to Lose Your Leader."

There are all sorts of ways to fail. Thousands of stories have been told about life's small and large tragedies. Physical things don't usually cause managers to fail. People do!

Our task is to identify the fundamental reasons why some people fail to get the management job done. I place the kinds of people who don't get the job done into two main categories:

People who don't really want the job,
and
people who can't handle the responsibility.

Some people know they don't want to be leaders, and they find themselves being promoted to a role of leadership because of circumstances. Some make it, some don't. Other people are not sure, and when given the chance to lead they discover that having to tell others what to do is just not for them. They aren't happy. In either case, the job doesn't get done.

There have been times when I've promoted very good workers to supervisory jobs, only to have them start displaying very disruptive behavior traits. Traits they didn't display before their promotion.

This puzzled me for years. Until I began to realize that the only reason this phenomenon makes any sense is that these otherwise good employees were just not happy being supervisors. Most of the time, this was buried deep in their subconscious minds. Abdication is one of the main causes of leadership failure.

I believe that many managers, some with great potential for success, often just give up, because they really don't want to be managers in the first place. Even though we tend to lump all of these people who don't succeed at management as losers, I don't think it's fair.

I believe that forcing someone to take a job that they really don't want to have doesn't help anyone. Why lose a great welder by trying to make him a welding foreman, when he really doesn't want to be one?

There is no shame in gracefully giving up the opportunity to assume a leadership role.

Management is not for everybody. However, I do firmly believe that anyone who really wants to be a good manager can be. The important thing to understand is that the same principles for developing successful working relationships will work for you whether you're the boss or not.

It is very important to understand that you don't have to be in management to be happy and successful.

Businesses need more workers than managers to begin with. All too often, a common practice is to terminate someone who wasn't able to handle a promotion.

The typical management thinking is that a person would probably lose respect and not be happy if they were returned to their old job in the same company.

I believe that thinking is seriously flawed. I never understood why you should terminate an otherwise good company employee? Why not let the person make the choice to return to a previously held job?

That's the kind of common situation I faced at the asphalt company, and I think the true story about my old friend Gene supports my way of thinking.

Gene was the local plant manager at the time I took over as the regional manager of the Louisiana asphalt operations. Try as he might, he just wasn't getting the job done.

Costs had skyrocketed, production was off, service was poor, and the angry union workers were preparing to strike.

I was named regional manager with the specific mandate to turn around the financial status of the money losing refinery, and the company president had agreed that I could make any changes and replace anyone that I thought I needed to.

My first inclination was that we probably needed a different plant manager. I knew that Gene was having serious personal problems, and, to say the least, he definitely was not a happy camper.

Gene had been with the company for many years, and he had been sent to Louisiana from a smaller, less complicated, refinery in Texas.

In essence, Gene had been promoted to the position as the Louisiana plant manager because he had done a good job at his previous plant back in Texas.

Instinctively, everybody understood that if Gene lost his job it would be because of me. Needless to say, I didn't think that I would be one of Gene's favorite people if I cost him his job.

Because he had been with the company for so long, I thought that I should at least give him a chance to remain at the Louisiana plant under my immediate supervision.

I gave him two choices. He could stay in Louisiana working under me, or he could go back to the smaller Texas plant, where he had come from. I think Gene's bags were packed before the day was over.

Nobody was ever so glad to go back home. I did him the biggest favor anyone had ever done for him in his whole life. When he got back to the Texas plant he did an even better job than he had done before he came to Louisiana.

To finish the story, Gene went back to Texas and I promoted another man as the refinery manager in Louisiana. Both of them did outstanding jobs and everyone was happy.

I'm happy to report that instead of Gene holding his loss of the Louisiana manager's job against me, he became one of my biggest fans in the company.

Each time I drove through Texas, he made sure I would stop at his plant just so he could take me out to dinner.

Gene belonged to that first group of people. He failed at leadership, simply because he really didn't want to be the manager of the Louisiana refinery. He wanted to be in Texas, where his home was, where he knew the people, and where he could once again feel good about his life.

Gene stayed with the company long after I left to go on to other challenges. He was still the manager of the Texas refinery at the time he finally retired.

Gene died a few years ago, but I'll always think of Gene as one of the important friends that helped me learn a few things along the way about serving people.

The second group of people who fail at management are those who want to be leaders, but can't handle the responsibilities that go with the territory. They go for the brass ring, only to drop it, while going around in endless circles getting nowhere. There's no free ride in business. You only get to keep riding as long as you're getting the job done.

Getting the job done means surviving in the toughest most highly competitive global market in history. Getting by today takes all of the resources you have, and constant improvement in everything you do.

Admittedly, there are a multitude of things that can keep a manager from making the grade. We're going to take a brief look at a few of the major organizational behavior issues that Street Smart Managers need to address.

For emphasis, I've put the operative words describing many of these management issues in bold type. The first, and by far the most critical, issue is your own personality.

As a manager or for that matter even if you're not a manager, the only person that you can really hope to control is yourself.

Many times people don't even know how to control themselves. They let their emotions override their intelligence. If you can't manage yourself, you can't possibly expect to manage others. When it comes to getting the job done, the place to start is definitely within you.

You need to be ready to assume control of the baton of leadership when it's handed to you. If you drop the stick, you lose the race. That means you have to believe that you can do what needs to be done. Above all, you need a good self-image. When it comes to trying to manage others, lack of confidence is: Enemy Number One.

A TIMELESS TIP

> **A manager with no respect has no influence.**

When you have a job to do, it's up to you to plan how you're going to do it. If every detail has to be planned out for you, then you're not a leader. You're just following someone else. Failure to plan adequately has doomed many a wannabe manager.

Closely associated with failing to plan is failing to adapt to changes. Failure at solving operating problems is another fatal detriment to getting the job done.

Certainly one of the main obstacles a manager faces is maintaining effective communications. Managers, who can't communicate, end up having to do everything.

Poor communication wrecks teamwork, and teamwork is the ultimate essential for getting a job done efficiently and effectively.

Managers who allow conflicts and harassment to permeate their workplace lose the respect of their workers, and will eventually lose control. People can always spot insecurity and fear of failure in a manager's personality.

With no teamwork, there is no concentration of effort. Without cooperation, most jobs become harder and harder to complete. Teamwork doesn't just call for bodies on the bench. It calls for the minds and hearts of all of the players.

Each member of a team must feel like a part of the team, and they must be empowered to contribute to the team's success. Managers who don't delegate effectively take away people's power to perform.

We've already talked about service being at the heart of a manager's job. Everyone in an organization provides a service to someone else. If an employee doesn't provide a needed service, the company doesn't need that employee.

I realize that I've addressed what seems like an awesome amount of responsibilities that a manager has to bear. Frustration with finding the time to handle all of these responsibilities, and succumbing to the stress of the responsibility are sure signs that a manager is headed for failure.

Goods and services are produced by people using all kinds of things. No matter what business you're in, you will have to deal with both people and things.

Managers, who can't coordinate the efforts of their people with the things they need to accomplish their work, will never achieve efficiency.

A TIMELESS TIP

> **Managers who fail to understand
> the service they provide
> will surely fail to provide it.**

Leaders who can't be trusted create no loyalty. Without loyalty, no one succeeds. Managers without morals have no ethical foundation. These kinds of managers generally fail to get the job done because they lose their credibility and respect.

No company can survive with poor motivation and low morale at any level. This is true from the top to the bottom.

Cheer up! Don't be discouraged by the list of problems we just discussed. They sound much worse than they are. Each and every one of these problems can usually be solved by ordinary thinking and caring people. People just like you and me. You'll find a practical answer to each of these problems in the following chapters.

The rest of this book is dedicated to helping those of you who have decided that you truly want to be successful leaders, and who are willing to accept the responsibility that goes along with making that critical decision.

In the introduction, I promised to divulge the two sure steps that will make you a success. We've already covered them, and you'll discover them over and over as we continue walking along the yellow brick road to success called:

Street Smart Management.

CHAPTER 5

"Get a Life"

> **If you don't like the person you see**
>
> **be the person you want to be**

I couldn't start this chapter without admitting that I consider myself a very, very, lucky person. I've been surrounded by happy, positive people all of my life.

My greatest piece of luck was being the last child of one of the most successful "people persons" that I have ever known. Like most good southern children, I lovingly called him "Daddy" until the day he died. Whenever I was smart enough to ask him for advice, he was always there. I was lucky to have him until he was 82 years old.

I also had the good fortune of being raised in a close-knit, loving, and supportive family, with five sisters and one brother. In addition, without a doubt, I certainly have the world's greatest and bravest stepmother. She married a man with seven children.

Like most other children, I did lots of things that I shouldn't have done, and there were times when I figured that just getting by in life was okay.

There were a few times when my father expressed painful disappointment in my poor choices for my behavior, and there's no denying that I deserved the guilt that I felt when I realized I had caused him emotional pain.

Nevertheless, he never once said that he was disappointed in me. He was only disappointed with the things that I had done or failed to do. He always corrected me with love.

The most important thing that I learned from my father was not something that he actually told me. It was something I observed from his constant example. My most valuable lesson for my life is simply this: Before you can expect to get other peoples' respect, you have to be able to respect yourself and respect them.

Without any fear of contradiction, I am proud to say that my father, John A. Zimmermann, was one of the most loved and universally respected men I've ever known. In my father's outlook on life, it wasn't necessary for us children to do anything more than to be ourselves and be happy.

He taught us the values of personal honesty and integrity, and the strength of dependability and independence. We learned to understand those enduring rock solid building blocks of happiness and success:

Faith, Hope, and Love.

I was born in the middle of the Great Depression, during the time when my father was State Director of the Louisiana Department of Recreation for the WPA.

Later, after World War II had started, he became the Executive Director of all of the U.S.O. service clubs operated by the N.C.C.S. throughout seven of the southern states.

After the big war ended, he found his final calling as a highly successful and respected charity fundraiser.

Over the years, my father directed numerous fund raising campaigns for local charities, including: The Community Chest, The United Fund, The Heart Fund, The United Negro College Fund, and The New Orleans Symphony, to name a few.

All of these organizations benefited greatly from his outstanding management skills. He also headed up building campaigns for a Jewish synagogue, a Catholic school, a major central-city hospital, and the Greater New Orleans Chamber of Commerce Building. After his first heart attack, he finally retired from fund raising at the age of 72.

Daddy never got rich. It never was his goal. His happiness was helping other people at being happy. When I look at the many buildings that he helped to build, I see lasting brick and mortar monuments to his unique leadership ability.

Corporate managers usually think pay, promotion, and job security are the three strongest employee-motivating forces there are. I have my doubts as to whether these forces really work even in the corporate world. They certainly can't motivate or even put fear in the hearts of volunteers. Volunteers aren't influenced by pay rates. They don't have a desire for promotion, and they don't have a fear of losing their jobs.

So, exactly how do you inspire an all-volunteer staff? Well, throughout his long fund raising career my father directed many successful all-volunteer campaign staffs, and Daddy simply practiced what he preached. He fully understood that the most valuable thing about most volunteer workers was that they were highly self-motivated. Their dedication and commitment was freely given and it was total. He just made sure he didn't get in their way.

All of my life, I saw my father living a very happy life, just helping other people to be happy and successful. I can report from personal observation, that the thousands of volunteers my father worked with, who raised millions and millions of dollars for others, never got one red cent for themselves.

Before my father died, he told me something I'll never forget. His exact words were these: "In all the years I've been in the fund raising business, I've never personally asked anyone for money." To me that statement was totally amazing. I can't remember my father ever directing a campaign that didn't meet or exceed its goal.

There's no doubt about it, Daddy knew the secret for getting others to do what had to be done. My father was a terrific role model for what I call a Street Smart Manager.

My second greatest stroke of luck was being handed the secret of happiness and success more than fifty years ago, although, like most of my childhood friends, I didn't realize it at the time.

The proven formula for a lifetime of success was sitting right in front of me every day, right on top of my old wooden school desk.

It was stamped into a thin piece of wood, just twelve inches long, imprinted with these eleven powerful words:

"Do Unto Others,
As You Would Have Them Do Unto You"

Well, there it is again, just as I promised, the key to the two-step formula for success. The "Golden Rule Ruler" was a gift to the schoolchildren of New Orleans. Thanks Coca-Cola!!! This most important formula for happiness has been proven, over, and over, and over again.

It's truly the essential ingredient for true success. It works for any endeavor you undertake. If you want to be a true winner, learn to follow the "Golden Rule."

The basic formula is simple, however, fully understanding why it works and learning how to use it to its fullest potential is a lifelong journey. I'm still learning something new about the practical side of the Golden Rule every day.

What does it take to make it work for you? First, it takes faith, to believe that the formula really works. It takes maintaining a perpetual hope that others will respond in kind, and when it begins to look like the Golden Rule is just a bunch of nice sounding words; it takes self-esteem and self-confidence to wait for results. I've never been disappointed.

Sometimes it's very difficult to understand why people do harmful things, and it's hard to forgive people who do things that make you feel hurt and mad. That's the reasons defensiveness and revenge are such powerful forces. People aren't perfect.

A TIMELESS TIP

> **Forgiving others
> lets you forgive you.**

Jealousy and resentment affect us everyday. Insecurity and withdrawal are common rational human reactions to perceived personal threats. The most common reason why people have problems accepting the "Golden Rule" philosophy is because they have very low self-esteem. Low self-esteem is synonymous with a poor self-image.

The reasons why different people have poor self-images differ greatly. Regardless of the source, basically the detrimental effects of poor self-images in the workplace are the same. Poor self-images cause problems no matter why or where they're found in the workplace.

All supervisors with low self-confidence generally exhibit some or all of the same kinds of dysfunctional behavior traits. They can be very timid, unsure of themselves, and unable to maintain discipline. Or, they can be ruthless, dictatorial, and judgmental. They put other people down, just to feel better about themselves. They can be negative and pessimistic.

A worker with a poor self-image is as much of a problem in the workplace as is a supervisor with a poor self-image. Workers with poor self-images exhibit depression, apathy, tardiness, absenteeism, paranoia, poor morale, and many other non-productive and disruptive tendencies. And they too can be offensive, and cause personal conflicts within a group.

Many managers simply pass off these kinds of traits in their employees as a "lack of motivation." They fail to see the root cause of these depressing personality traits. They only see the symptoms. They don't see the fundamental insecurity that low self-esteem generates. It is insecurity that is the real problem.

All of these types of problematic employee behavior traits can cause serious management problems, whether found in supervisors or workers.

I've always tried to help people out with their personal problems. I don't think I'm unusual in that regard. Most people will respond when they think someone needs help. So at times, when I thought I could help someone become more effective at work, I tried to help them with their personal problems. I still do.

But, I'll have to confess that trying to help certain people occasionally caused me problems that I really didn't need, especially when I mistakenly thought I could help change someone's basic behavior.

In all my years in management, I've never succeeded at changing anyone with self-induced, self-destructive, and self-perpetuated personality traits. People can only be helped when they want to be helped. I've learned that lesson the hard way. The only personality that you can really control or change is your own. Your own self-image and your own personal behavior patterns set the tone for your success.

My advice is this: Never try to change a person's personality, and don't try to force them to do things they don't want to do. That's not a manager's job. A manager's job is simply getting people to do what needs to be done, in order to achieve a worthwhile common goal.

A manager usually isn't a trained social worker. Don't try to be one. Leave that important job to the professionals.

A Street Smart Manager understands that we don't live in a perfect world. We live in a human world, and managers must learn to deal with human imperfection. In the real business world, most people have to be dealt with just as they are. Whenever a person was struggling to handle a certain job, I always attempted to transfer them to another job that they could handle. It didn't always work.

Regretfully, deciding that you have to fire someone is usually a very difficult situation. Many managers feel guilty when they determine that they just can't work with someone any longer.

Terminating someone is never a pleasant task. It's a part of a manager's job that you won't like, but in many cases, it's got to be done.

It's absolutely essential for a manager to know whom to hire, and whom to fire. If your decision to fire someone is based on truth, and it's in the best interest of the company, you'll have no real reason to feel guilty.

Sometimes a manager can inspire someone, and then that person goes out and does great things. But, in truth, the real motivation to do great things only comes from within the person themselves.

86

On the other hand, it's important to remember that it is much easier for a manger to de-motivate someone than to inspire them. Someone told me that de-motivate is not a word, so I'll give it my own definition.

De-motivation is a word I use to describe the process of causing others to suppress their own natural motivation.

If you don't think you deserve happiness, then how can you really expect to believe that others deserve happiness? If you don't think you're worthwhile, how can you expect to believe that others are worthwhile? If you're a pessimist, how can you ever expect to agree with an optimist?

Routinely, even people with a normal positive and healthy self-image have times when they doubt their own worth. Psychologists call this state of doubt "depression." Everyone suffers from some degree of depression at certain times in his or her lives. It's normal.

Generally, depression is mild and short lived for most people. The real danger point is when depression degenerates into the depths of despair.

People with very low self-esteem tend to think of themselves as failures. They aren't very happy, so they reason that they must be failures. They develop negative and pessimistic attitudes. This painful state of mind doesn't have to be. It's a waste of time.

Everyone has the ability to be as happy and successful as he or she wants to be. They only have to believe in themselves and make the right choices.

If you don't like the person you see, then be the person you want to be.

Can I tell you exactly how to improve your own self-image? Not really. Not any more than you could tell me exactly how to improve my self-image. I would like to think that I could, but everyone has to solve that problem for him or herself. You have to find your own reasons to truly believe that you have a fundamental right to a full life and the pursuit of happiness.

As I said before, I'm lucky because it's easy for me. I was taught to believe that God created us as unique individuals, and that we have a right to happiness. I believe we have the opportunity and an obligation to get the most out of life.

If we could prove that there was a God, we wouldn't need faith. When my faith is strong, my confidence is very positive. But, my self-esteem constantly wanes in a direct relationship to the dark depths of my doubts.

Faith is frustrating. It takes faith to have faith. I've found that my faith always needs reinforcement, and that the reinforcement is totally up to me.

Some people say that believing in God is just a crutch. So what? God works for me, so I can't worry about what others say. I've just decided to be happy. That's it, and that's enough for me.

Although, let's not just rely on claiming any God given rights to life, liberty, and the pursuit of happiness.

Let's look at the existence of individual rights from the standpoint of pure and simple logic.

I certainly wouldn't have to care about anybody else's rights if I didn't have any rights of my own. Why should I? It wouldn't make sense. What would make me believe that any other person had more right to life and happiness than I had? Nothing at all!

Any society without individual rights would be chaotic. Luckily, our country's founding fathers understood this basic proposition: In order to have an orderly world, everyone needs to have the same basic rights.

The greatest value of our United States Constitution is that all people, even those who don't even believe in God, have the same rights to pursue their happiness as everyone else. Nobody is better than anybody else is. Furthermore, thank God, everyone is uniquely different from everybody else.

On the practical side of my argument for individual rights, I absolutely find no valid reason for anyone to have a poor self-image. A poor self-image doesn't help anyone. It's not good for you, and it certainly doesn't help anyone associated with you.

If you're getting ready to open your own business, or if you're already in management, then I'd say that your self-image should be in pretty good shape. It's up to you to keep it that way.

However, if your patience is wearing thin, or if you're starting to take your frustrations out on your workers, your spouse, and your children; and you find that you're not having very much fun at work, it's time to give your self-image a close examination.

Don't wait for somebody else to do something about your unhappiness. It could be too late. An honest diagnosis may call for some real self-improvement effort. You may even seek professional therapy.

It is totally impossible for me to over-emphasize the powerful influence of healthy, positive self-images in the workplace. Self-confidence is the real cornerstone of successful leadership. It affects every aspect of the working environment.

Trying to be a successful manager, without first developing a positive self-image, is like trying to learn to swim when you're afraid of the water. You might learn to splash around and stay afloat, but you'll never enjoy swimming, and you'll surely never win an Olympic Gold Medal for the 100-meter backstroke.

The simple truth is this: If you don't have a good self-image, you certainly won't succeed at winning with the "Golden Rule."

People that have good self-images aren't afraid to share their knowledge with others. They aren't afraid to give someone else credit for doing a good job. They're great people to work with and to work for, and they invariably surround themselves with winners.

Any firm that wants to survive in the serious game of business competition needs to have leaders who are winners. Companies need managers who can run with the ball, and score the points. They need managers who can tough it out, and stay in the game. Street Smart Managers never give up. They're all-around winners.

This chapter is titled **"Get a Life"** because that's the ultimate street slang put-down for life's losers.

One of the things that I realized early in my working life was that the best way for me to get ahead was to work for someone who knew more than I did, and who wasn't afraid to teach me what he or she knew.

People with positive self-images love themselves enough to live life to the fullest. They enjoy other people and the feel good whenever people they know do well. They're not jealous.

By and large, I've been very lucky to work with many people that taught me things I couldn't easily learn from a book. They showed me things that would have taken me years to learn from making my own mistakes.

I'm indebted to each and every one of them. They showed me that management can be fun, and that serving others in the role of a manager is a great and rewarding life. It's never dull. It's always full of new opportunities, challenges, and rewards.

In the coming chapter, we'll look at why Franklin D. Roosevelt said:

"The only thing we have to fear is fear itself."

We'll also see how open communications eliminates most of the dark shadows of ignorance that create fear among your workers, and we'll explore the basics of effective business communications.

CHAPTER 6

"Yes or No"

We all learned to listen before we learned to talk, but sometimes we forget the sequence.

"To be? Or not to be?" What kind of silly question is that? To be! That's the only good answer on the great stage of business. When it comes to being, being you and having high self-esteem are absolute requirements.

At drama, romance, and intrigue, Shakespeare was among the greatest. But good old William couldn't cut the mustard in today's world of fast paced communications.

Personally, I've never seen a really well run business organization that didn't have a fairly high level of effective communications, and operating a business is certainly a social endeavor.

Conversely, I've also never seen a company with relatively poor communications that was well managed. Effective communications is the key to successful leadership.

In all social environments, the ability to understand your own internal motivations and the ability to adequately communicate your true feelings and ideas to others is essential.

Business communications may not be glamorous and romantic, but the ability to express one's thoughts is extremely important to everyone that works for a living. It is especially crucial to everyone that supervises others.

The subject of business communications must include all types of written messages and verbal intercourse among and between working people. I divide all business communications into two main broad categories:

Operational
and
Promotional

For my purposes, I further divide all operational communications according to their three basic functions:

Instruction
Information
Persuasion.

My experience tells me that sending and receiving all types of communications requires the same level of attention. All types of managers, at all levels of a business, should follow the same basic guidelines for all of their internal and external communications.

However, writing sales letters and creating advertising copy is another area of communications altogether different from routine internal correspondence.

Some of the restraints placed on institutional communications don't apply to the fine art of writing good advertising copy. We'll leave that task to the professional copy writers.

Primarily, I'm going to confine my thoughts in this chapter to communications by and between superiors and their subordinates. Mastering this particular form of communications is the key to getting things done.

I'll be the first to admit that I haven't always been totally successful at getting others to understand my own messages. Then again, no one is. However, I can tell you, with ironclad certainty, that every time I've failed to communicate my instructions and ideas successfully, it has cost me big bucks.

Luckily, so far it has only cost me time and money. Sometimes, a failure to communicate can cost you much more. It can be deadly.

I think I have learned some very valuable lessons over the many years of trying to get my messages across more effectively. I'm confident that you too will reap some lasting benefit from the fundamental observations and thoughts that I've recorded in this book.

There is no substitute for credibility. There's no easy road to recovery once it's lost. People who can't be trusted to tell the truth in little things are seldom trusted to tell the truth about anything.

Let me say this right up front. None of the other suggestions that I offer to you in this book will even come close to being as important as my first piece of communications advice:

In everything you write and
everything you say;
tell the truth,
the whole truth, and
nothing but the truth.

Just consider this very common example: You've probably experienced being told that someone wasn't in, when you knew very well that they were right there at the time you called. It happens to me all the time.

Do you ever have doubts about those bosses who ask their secretary to lie for them by telling you that they weren't available to come to the phone when they really were? How do you feel about that person's credibility?

Do you feel rejected when someone doesn't return your calls? I do, and I distrust that person's sincerity. They lose their credibility. I have a hard time dealing with people that I know can't be trusted.

So my second most important piece of advice is this:

Be sure to listen,
before you have to lament.

The world is full of people still singing this sad old refrain:

"I sure wish I would have listened to what they said."

We all learned to listen before we learned to talk, but sometimes we forget the sequence. Good listeners not only learn a lot, they also never run out of things to talk about. Good listeners always ask questions about things that interest the other person in the conversation. Good conversationalists realize that when they let other people have chances to talk, then they only had to hold up one half of the conversation.

My third simplified recommendation for maintaining good communication is fun and easy:

Add a little humor to your conversation.

The very nature of a manager's job is to deal with problems and mistakes that people make, and nobody really likes criticism.

When you have to talk to someone about a personal behavior problem, a little humor helps to soften the blow.

Humor makes people laugh and feel good. Keeping business communications strictly business doesn't mean being dull, boring, harsh, or hostile. Street Smart Managers always try to be positive, exciting, and inspirational.

In this chapter, we're going to take a closer look at what constitutes truly effective supervisory communications. Hopefully, this review will help you to improve your effectiveness at both sending and receiving messages.

The **Medium** and the **Message** are the two principle factors we must always consider when discussing supervisory communications.

The Medium: The medium is simply the physical means by which your message is delivered.

The array of media that is available to you today is almost unbelievable. Further complicating matters, in our futuristic electronic world the choice of media is constantly improving at a faster and faster rate.

It wasn't that long ago when a hand delivered paper telegram was the surest and fastest way to get a written message from one location to another. I remember those times very well.

As a teenager, I once had a summer job as a Western Union telegram delivery boy, bicycle and all. Initially, I was assigned to the central business district office, and I delivered telegrams on foot to offices in many of the high rise buildings in downtown New Orleans. Later, I was then transferred to a branch office, and from there I delivered my telegrams by bicycle.

My longest trip was from uptown New Orleans to the little town of Westwego, Louisiana. Westwego was all the way on the other side of the Mississippi river from New Orleans.

It was more than twenty miles round-trip, and I had to peddle there and back over the Huey P. Long Bridge. The old steel bridge was steep, narrow, and very high. It took me four hours to deliver that one telegram. My poor skinny legs hurt for days.

After delivering a few more telegrams to other out-of-the-way places like Westwego, I was never so glad for school to start again the next fall.

Today you can FAX a hardcopy message to almost anywhere in the world in just minutes. Everything has changed so drastically in such a short period of time. Even the word hardcopy is a fairly new word.

The terms that define the media of today are extensive: Satellites, fiber-optic cables, laser printers, cellular phones, and two-way video phones, just to name a few.

However, one thing never changes: No matter which medium you use, it still takes at least one person to originate a message and at least one to receive it.

It's obvious that all people are still not equally capable of sending and receiving messages via all types of media. Use the wrong medium and your message might not get through.

People wishing to communicate a message to someone else must choose the most effective means of transmitting their message to the intended receiver.

Many people say that the safest and most effective policy for giving instructions is to always put them in writing. In most cases that's true, but not necessarily in all cases.

This story about my friend Robert is an excellent example of such a case.

Robert worked with me at the asphalt refinery. He was in his late thirties, and was working as a laborer. A laborer was someone who did everything in the plant that nobody else wanted to do. The truth is: Robert did the dirty work. He was at the lowest wage scale in the plant.

Most of the time Robert was assigned to general housekeeping duties. He cleaned up the ugly sticky spills, helped the maintenance crew, loaded delivery trucks, and did many other menial and thankless jobs.

Robert would do anything you asked him to do, and he generally did it well. He stuck with a job until it was done.

Even though he was one of our most dependable and hardest working employees, he never tried to advance any higher than his position as a common laborer.

Luckily, we accidentally found out why he never tried out for a higher paying job. One day we learned that Robert couldn't read nor write.

Surprisingly, Robert could count and he could match the number of cartons he loaded with the written numbers on a shipping order. He could read numbers well enough to load a truck from a shipping ticket by himself, but he couldn't read anything else.

Because he couldn't read, he was afraid that he couldn't even qualify for common labor work. As many illiterates do, he hid his handicap well.

100

After the plant manager found out that Robert couldn't read, he simply had the shift supervisors give Robert verbal instructions.

After he changed the medium to suit Robert's needs, the plant manager could then use Robert on more skilled jobs.

Robert became one of the best production workers we had. Since he was more productive, he was then able to earn more money. Everybody won! Robert's communication problem wasn't that he couldn't understand the message; he simply wasn't able to use the medium of the written word. Sadly, this is not uncommon in today's labor market.

There seems to be an opinion among human resource personnel that many of our schools are not providing our children with a sufficient education for today's global marketplace.

While the actual number of people in the workplace who can't read basic writing might be relatively small, the number of people who can't fully comprehend the meaning of what they read seems to be growing.

These kinds of people need more effective verbal support. They need more details and more extensive explanations of what needs to be done.

Dealing with poorly educated workers is an ever present and growing problem for today's manager. More and more, using multi-media is a necessity.

It's safe to say that no matter what type of media you choose, good verbal communication is almost always necessary to supplement the best of written communications. For example: If I were explaining the contents of this book to you verbally, it might make more sense.

The Message: The message is simply the thought you wish to convey.

Just as the wrong medium can prevent someone from receiving your message, trying to send a poorly organized message can overshadow even the best of the media.

Writing business correspondence is a routine management duty, which most people in the working world have to fulfill at some time or another.

Letters and memos fall under the heading of general business correspondence. The best writing tip I can offer is to invite you to join my Four C Club.

Membership is free and there are only four rules. The by-laws are simple and easy to follow. The four rules state that all written business correspondence should be:

Clean,
Clear,
Candid, and
Concise

Clean requires keeping your writings simple and easy to understand. Don't include ideas that are not necessary to the basic message you are trying to convey.

Clear calls for letters and memos to be logical. They must make sense, and not be confusing. The sequence of information in your letter should follow an easily understandable order.

Candid is self-evident. Never try to mislead by saying something other than what you really mean. Be straightforward and passionate about what you are saying.

Concise means short. It's is better to send a series of short letters rather than one long complicated letter.

Once you know your first letter has been received and fully understood, then send a follow-up letter making your next point.

Letters and memos expressing one main topic are more effective than those containing several unrelated and possibly confusing topics.

Since business writing accounts for only a minor portion of the responsibilities of a manager, I have devoted the remainder of this chapter to discussing several common areas of concern about instructional and informational messages.

Even though we all must be both senders and receivers for most means of communicating, in business settings there are two broad classes of people: 1) Those people who are primarily **Senders** and 2) those who are ordinarily the **Receivers.**

Recently, I talked with scores of people falling into each of these two classes of employees while conducting some basic management effectiveness research. I asked the different classes of respondents to tell me how they regarded the effectiveness of the overall communications within their companies. I'm sorry to report that the general response was not positive.

These front-line managers, who routinely do most of the instructional sending in a company, usually felt that higher management's record for communicating with them was generally poor. As expected, they thought that their own communication effectiveness was much better. Personal bias in their favor was evident.

On the other side of the coin, my research findings indicated that most of the workers, who generally receive instructions; often indicated that they felt the company's information system was not very effective at any level.

This research also showed that the typical mid-level senders listed lack of trust, lack of support, and a lack of complete information from higher management as their most serious concerns.

Secondly, they stated that they felt that their subordinates lacked the basic ability to understand them.

Other Sender concerns included: Poor information flow from the bottom up, little cooperation between managers on the same level, interference from the grapevine, and fear of telling higher management bad news.

In other words, most of the Senders believed that the problem with communications was not with them.

Information receivers saw the problems in reverse. They felt that managers didn't take the time to give them complete information. They felt that they didn't have the freedom to ask management for clarification when communications weren't clear. They didn't trust what management told them, and they didn't think management even cared about receiving any feedback on what the workers thought.

A TIMELESS TIP

Look - Listen - Learn

Having acknowledged some of the more commonly seen problems in communications, it brings us to my law of **"Dialogue Direction."**

Just as in every other function of leadership, having the authority and the privilege of sending messages carries with it the full responsibility for making sure your messages are completely understood.

Good managers fully understand that the only purpose for business communications is to serve the company. Good leaders must have self-confidence in their own ability to communicate. Without displaying self-confidence, it is absolutely impossible to gain the confidence of a fearful receiver.

In the following chapter we'll look closely at the fine art of sending and receiving all types of business operational messages.

CHAPTER 7

"Dialogue Direction"

Listening is just as important as speaking

I think I made up the law of "Dialogue Direction." But, since I'm not totally sure that someone else didn't come up with something similar before me, give them the credit if you know their name. It's no big deal.

The law of Dialogue Direction governs the exchange of instructions, facts, ideas, and opinions within a company. The direction of dialogue specifically refers to the responsibility for making sure that all types of messages have been sent and received completely and accurately.

The flow of dialogue or its direction in a business is generally downward, from top management to the lowest level employee.

The full and final force of responsibility always rests with the person giving the instructions, not the person receiving them.

This undeniable fact can never change: The responsibility for the entire communications effectiveness of any organization is always from the top down.

Generally, in both sending and receiving situations, the higher the level of authority, the greater the responsibility for insuring effective communications.

In a practical sense, the law of dialogue direction simply dictates that the person giving the instructions is responsible for making sure that the person who needs the instructions gets them completely and accurately.

The law of **Dialogue Direction** can also be expressed like this:

The person with the greater ability to understand has the greater responsibility for insuring that an understanding has been reached.

It's true that adequate feedback during all instructional communications must be both upward and downward, but the full responsibility for insuring that a subordinate's feedback of the instructions is both correct and complete still falls on the higher authority.

The person sending the message is the one who knows what the message is; therefore the sender is responsible for making sure that the one receiving the message understands it. In all kinds of persuasive communications, the one who is trying to do the convincing has the total responsibility to make the selling point.

Tell your listener what you want them to understand, and then ask them to repeat what you said. Listen to their answer. If they didn't understand the first time, tell them again, and again, until they do.

Sometimes, drawing simple pictures or diagrams of what you're trying to explain helps greatly. There's a real reason why a picture is sometimes worth a thousand words. People are very visual.

If they still don't understand, maybe what you're trying to explain isn't understandable. Or at least it might not be understandable to the person you're trying to explain it to.

Try explaining it to someone else. If they can't understand you either, the problem could be you.

Is it you, or is it them? It doesn't really matter at the time, for in either case you should never ask someone to do something that they don't fully understand. It can have serious and dangerous consequences.

Both Toastmasters' International and the National Speakers Association, two of the premier organizations dedicated to enhancing the art of public speaking, advocate that Listening is just as important as Speaking.

The necessity for good listening skills is especially critical in the supervisory field.

The best system for making sure that someone understands your instructions is to simply ask them if they understand. If they say they do, ask them to repeat your instructions. Listen carefully, and if they repeat your instructions completely and accurately, then at least you know that they knew what you said at the time you said it.

This procedure surely doesn't insure that your employee will remember your instructions correctly at a later time, but it's absolutely certain that if your employee can't repeat your instructions correctly at the time you first give them, then he or she definitely won't be able to carry out your instructions correctly at a later time.

When I was a student pilot at Greenville Air Force Base in Mississippi, one of my fellow classmates lost his life because of a fatal failure to communicate.

The Air Force uses an "announce and respond" system for going through a preflight checklist. The pilot reads the item to be accomplished out loud, and either the pilot or co-pilot, when there are two pilots on board, responds when the activity has been completed.

It's an excellent system, as long as it's followed faithfully. Unfortunately, just one lax moment of missed communications cost a fellow student pilot his life.

The fatal accident happened during a two ship formation takeoff. While trying to take off in the second position he didn't read and acknowledge two critical little words during his preflight checklist: "Flaps Down."

Using flaps allows a plane to takeoff at a lower speed than when not using flaps. The wing flaps give an airplane added lift on takeoff.

In formation flying, the pilot in the second plane (the wing man) doesn't normally look at any instruments inside of his own cockpit. He looks only at the lead plane, and does exactly what the lead plane does. A wing man has to have total faith in the lead pilot.

In the accident that killed my classmate, the pilot in the lead plane had his flaps down twenty degrees on the takeoff roll. He cleared the end of the runway at the normal takeoff speed for twenty degrees of flaps without any problems.

Sadly, when the second pilot tried to break ground on takeoff at the same time, and at the same speed as the lead plane, he didn't make it.

Even though he was at the same takeoff speed as the lead plane, without the twenty degrees of flaps, the plane didn't have enough lift to stay in the air. He crashed and burned right off the end of the runway.

The simple mistake of forgetting those two little words cost a promising young man his life. Sometimes life teaches us some very hard lessons.

Later on, when I became an instructor pilot myself, I remembered that deadly lesson on the results of failing to communicate accurately and completely. I decided I definitely didn't want to be another grim statistic in life's final exam grade book. Losing a little time and money is one thing, losing my life was something else.

So, whenever I was instructing a new pilot, I would meticulously explain a critical maneuver to my student before I actually demonstrated it. Then, as I would be flying through it, I would explain it once again. After I finished a demonstration, I would make the student explain it to me in detail. He had to explain each step that I took, and tell me why I did it. He couldn't attempt to fly it until he could verbally explain the total maneuver.

Of course, this technique didn't insure that a student had either the manual dexterity or the mental skills necessary to actually fly an airplane.

I think I can say that there is no way that a person could learn to fly a plane if he couldn't at least understand the theory of flight. Luckily, most business communications are not that crucial. But, when your life is on the line, one misunderstanding could be one too many.

Bankruptcy is the equivalent of an early death in business, and the dead-end road to bankruptcy is littered with the rubble of broken communications.

Supervisors must learn to skillfully handle all three of the basic forms of communications in the management environment, namely:

Instructional, Informational, and Persuasive.

Informational communication flows from the person with the information to the person who needs to have the information.

However, the full responsibility for understanding and utilizing the information received is on the shoulders of the higher authority.

This does not relieve the person giving the information from the responsibility of trying to transmit it using the best of their ability. As a person, whether a supervisor or someone who is being supervised, the most important thing for you to know is this: **You need to know when you don't know what you need to know.**

If you don't understand what you're being told, keep asking and listening until you understand it, or you determine that the information is flawed, incomplete, or inaccurate. In that case the information is perhaps useless.

If you want to be a good communicator, you have to learn to listen and ask questions.

All companies have both a formal and an informal communication network. Both networks generally run along the same paths as both the official and the functional leadership channels within the company.

I describe these major avenues of communication as the **Mainline** and the informal **Grapevine**. Mainline communications within any organization is the easiest to describe, but it's not necessarily easy to control.

A formal business communications system is generally comprised of written, verbal, and visual forms of communications. It includes such formal things as policy statements, inter-office memos, company letters, house organs, advertising copy, publicity pieces, and generally anything that is generated by anyone in any kind of official capacity with a company.

As I've pointed out, the formal line of communication presents problems in several areas. However, it does have one very important advantage over the informal conduit of company information, and that is in most cases, all formal communications can be traced back to the original source.

Even though the formal communication system can't always guarantee the complete flow of information from the top to the bottom, problems with formal written communication can usually be corrected by issuing additional written statements.

Sometimes, as the flow proceeds down through the full range of formal channels of communication, important portions of intended information can get left out

In some cases, it inadvertently comes to a complete stop as the flow of information travels from the top to the bottom. Some levels of an organization never get the word.

In my experience, the only way to know if the formal communication system is working properly is to institute a company-wide announcement acknowledgment system.

In order to be valid, every formal type of acknowledgment system must include every recipient, from the very top to the very bottom.

On the informal side of the information channels, otherwise known as the Grapevine, information is totally outside of management's control.

This doesn't mean that the grapevine can't be a very valuable management tool. However, you do need to understand its limitations, and be very careful how you use it. Actually, management is an integral part of the grapevine.

An astute management team uses the grapevine as a source of information and feedback about employee attitudes and reactions. Take caution, the grapevine has to be closely monitored to guard against acting on bad information.

Walter J. Lambert, a good and dear friend, told me one of the best grapevine stories that I've ever heard. I was truly blessed to have known Walter, for he was always happy, a gifted and self-made man. Walter died a few years ago, at the age of 76.

Walter started working full time at the age of twelve, shortly after his father died. His first job was helping to deliver fresh baked bread at three o'clock in the morning. In the 1920's, hot bread was delivered to people's houses every morning.

After delivering his last loaf each morning he would walk to school and attend class for the rest of the day. Walter worked the bread truck in his little home town of Garyville, Louisiana until he finished high school.

Later, by the time World War II had started, Walter had learned to weld, and he had gotten a job building Liberty Ships in New Orleans.

Since he held a job critical to the war effort and was already married with a child to support, he wasn't drafted into the army.

The war years were tough economic times for everyone, so he worked two full-time welding jobs every day, at two competing New Orleans shipyards.

He worked the early shift at one yard and the late shift at the other, seven days a week. Of course, he didn't see his family very often, except on occasional holidays.

One year, during the time he was working at both shipyards, Thanksgiving was nearing and he thought it would be nice to have a rare family dinner, with a fat turkey and all of the trimmings.

When he asked his early shift foreman whether the company was going to give turkeys to the workers, his foreman said he didn't know. His foreman said that he didn't think so, because they had never done it before. At

Walter's request, he agreed to ask the big boss about it anyway.

That evening, when Walter arrived at his second job, he asked the night-shift foreman if that company was going to give turkeys. The second foreman told him that as far as he knew the company never gave turkeys.

So he told that supervisor: "Well, my day supervisor at the other yard told me that he was going to ask the boss over there to give us turkeys."

Naturally, his second shift foreman couldn't be outdone, so he also told him he would check with his boss about giving turkeys for Thanksgiving.

The next morning he told his first shift foreman that his night shift foreman was also planning to ask his company to give all the employees turkeys for Thanksgiving. The baited trap was set.

Walter said that he received two big Thanksgiving turkeys that year. He ate one turkey at home, with his wife and daughter, and gave the other turkey to his mother. Now that's a tasty story.

A TIMELESS TIP

> **Use the Three T's.**
> **Tell – Tell – Tell**

I'm glad Walter got his turkeys, but no manager should ever attempt to achieve a goal by giving misleading information. Don't be tempted to start rumors. They'll usually return to haunt you.

From a management standpoint, Walter's story is really a story about taking action based on incomplete information. As it turned out, each company did give turkeys that year, so it ended up being true. After the fact, that is.

The most critical aspect of communication between a manager and the people whom they work with is honesty. Good personal relations and mutual understandings don't exist without honesty. I'm sure you've heard this wise old saying:

**"You only get one chance
to make a good first impression."**

Well now, here's a similar admonition that fits communications very well: When you tell your first lie, kiss your credibility good-bye.

When you say no, mean no!
When you say yes, mean yes!

Don't give any ifs, ands, or buts. Just say: "Yes" or "No." Anything else is less than the truth. Total honesty is absolutely essential in all communications.

There's another dangerous old saying: "What you don't know can't hurt you." Well, that may be true in love, but believe me; it's certainly not true in business. What you don't know can hurt you, and it usually does. Telling half-truths and not telling vital truths are examples of dishonesty by omission.

Everyone in a company doesn't necessarily need to know everything about the inner workings of the company's management and finances.

There are certain things that the employees have no right and no need to know. Some people are actually better off not knowing certain information.

Knowing when to withhold information requires good judgment. But, in all cases, not telling someone something that they really do need to know is a form of dishonesty.

Good conversation is a very dynamic activity, it shouldn't be rigid. It requires give and take on each side. Good conversation calls for an active exchange of ideas and information.

Dialogue is a two-way street. Asking a person a non-threatening question is a splendid way of stimulating conversation. Most people have lots to say about the things they know the best. People will think you are a brilliant conversationalist if you keep them talking about themselves, and other things they know more about than you.

Knowing how to react to other people in a conversation is essential. A good conversation requires flexibility. Friendly conversations help relieve job stress. They can be used to pass on general information, or just to pass time.

A TIMELESS TIP

> **Don't say "yes" and don't say "no,"
> when what you really mean is
> "I don't know."**

The acronym **MESSAGES** briefly outlines eight useful suggestions for making instructions and informative communications more effective:

Effective business communicating involves preparation. Whether you're giving detailed job instructions, or giving out general information, you need to know exactly what you want to say before you say it.

When you're seeking information, you need to know exactly what you want to find out, so that you can ask the right questions. When you're trying to convince someone to accept your point of view, you need to be prepared to present your ideas in an orderly, persuasive, and passionate manner.

The ideas from my **Four C** writing guide are included within **MESSAGES**, my extended formula offered for improving the effectiveness of all forms of daily communications, especially in an operational business setting.

For in-person, spoken, instructional, informational, and persuasive communicating, I have added a few additional guidelines which reflect the sensory aspects of voice inflection, body language, volume, and tempo.

MEANINGFUL

This first hint fits both instructive and informative communicating equally well. It's a general suggestion, useful for helping managers make sure that the things they say are in the best interest of the company, and therefore themselves.

When speaking with the authority of the company, it's absolutely imperative for you to speak effectively and responsibly.

The basic essence of communicating is sending and receiving of a meaningful message. A message is meaningful if it is necessary to achieve a specific intention. Meaningful messages are simply intended to produce a desired response and some action. Meaningful does call for presenting the intention of the sender in a candid, straight-forward manner.

Don't confuse your intent to be meaningful with actually getting the desired results intended. From the sender's standpoint, a message can be meaningful even when the receiver makes no positive response to it, or takes no action at all.

Whether or not a message is beneficial or harmful, pleasant or unpleasant, good news or bad, acted upon or ignored, is not germane to the state of being meaningful.

Managers should never have a hidden agenda. Some people like to play the dangerous game of trying to use reverse psychology. I strongly advocate that business should be fun, but it's not a child's guessing game.

Frequently, a message is truly meant to embarrass someone or to put them down. There is no place for this kind of demeaning message or malicious gossip in a business setting.

Self-assured managers don't talk down to others. They don't need to. Good leaders have good and valid reasons for everything they write or say.

When you go swinging on the company grapevine, always say positive things about your company, and good things about your fellow workers.

Managers should always welcome conversation with their workers. In fact, small talk is very meaningful when it helps put the receiver in a more receptive mood for receiving a negative message. This old 1940's tune says it best:

**Accentuate the positive
eliminate the negative.**

EXPLICIT

Explicit can be described as definitive, specific, and clear. Being explicit is an all important aspect of all kinds of communicating. Always try to say exactly what you mean.

You may be sending a message to a large number of people all at the same time, but remember, your message will always be received by each person as they individually perceive it. Rarely will any two people interpret any one message in exactly the same way.

It is also important to realize that words and phrases mean different things to different people. People from different countries, different states, different cities, and even different neighborhoods, all have their own special words and phrases. The responsibility for being precise is up to the person giving the instructions. Be sure to use those words and phrases that your workers understand.

Most managers do pretty well with the who, what, when, and where. It's telling the "how" and the "why" that give them the most problems.

A very serious management problem stems from giving people instructions to do a job without giving them an adequate explanation of how and why it should be undertaken and accomplished. Just telling someone what you want them to do may not be enough.

If you don't want someone to use their own judgment for deciding when and how to accomplish a task, then make sure you tell them how and why they should do the job your way.

The missing link in most chains of communication is the WHY.

Yes! Yes! Yes! I know and I agree that there will be times when you won't have time to tell someone the "why."

However, the times when you can't at least give a short explanation of the reason why something should be done should be few and far between.

If you never have time to tell people why it's important to do a job, something is wrong somewhere. Even in real emergencies, explaining the "why-factor" generally helps solve the problem better and faster.

Rudyard Kipling gave us an excellent set of rules for making communications explicit. Remember these famous lines from the Elephant's Child:

I keep six honest serving-men
They taught me all I knew
Their names are What and Why and When
And How and Where and Who

SIMPLE

Simple should not be confused with short. Proper length is an important factor, but not for simplicity's sake.

You must say everything that is necessary to get your point across. Just don't say things that have nothing to do with getting your point across. Some people can move from doing one thing to another so fast that it appears that they are able to do several things at one time. That's only an illusion.

123

In reality, people can only actually comprehend one thing at a time. You can confuse people by trying to combine too many separate ideas into the same message.

SENSIBLE

Simple and sensible may sound like two words that mean the same thing; nevertheless, there is an important and distinct difference between the two words when it comes to communicating.

Sensible relates to the critical need for an orderly flow of information. Your orders and instructions must be easy to understand. Give information in a logical sequence.

Statements that are rambling and disorderly will confuse the listener. Even in cases where reaching the desired result only requires undertaking a simple sequence of activities, you might have problems when operating instructions are not in an easily understandable order.

Keeping your messages simple and sensible doesn't necessarily imply that your communications should always be confined to only one principle point.

However, most people are more capable of receiving several discrete messages when they are given in a series of understandable individual transmissions.

The idea is to make sure that each major point is presented in a simplified and sensible manner, before moving to the next point you wish to make.

However, there is something to be said about keeping the number of points you are trying to make to a minimum.

As a suggestion, three major points in any one message seems to be a reasonable limit.

ACCURATE

My definition of management or more precisely, my definition of leadership holds true for any level of management. I describe leadership as:

"Helping people to do what needs to be done."

Notice that my definition does not state: "Getting people to do what <u>you</u> want them to do."

The variation in these two definitions of leadership gives us an example of how even minor differences in intended meaning can affect communication.

It isn't what a supervisor personally wants done that's important. What is important is what the supervisor needs to have done, in order to reach the company's goals.

Supervisors should always have the same agenda as the company. We all know that's not always the case. All instructions must accurately portray what is necessary for achieving the overall goals and welfare of the company.

I'll carry that thought one step further, and I'll say without any fear of contradiction: Unless supervisors know exactly what their company's goals are, they can't possibly determine what needs to be done to reach those goals.

This example of the two definitions of leadership may be splitting hairs to some readers; still, as we'll see later, accuracy is critically important to achieving successful managerial communication.

The total responsibility for maintaining accurate communications starts from the highest level of management and flows downward. Truthfulness and completeness are enormously essential for effective communication. There is no substitute for truth.

Everything you write or say must be completely true. Not only does telling the truth safeguard your reputation, it's much less stressful than trying to remember lies. You don't have to remember the truth.

There is a little room for discretion when it comes to completeness. However, as I said before, use caution on this point: There are times when it's for someone's benefit that they don't know the whole story. Leaving something out of a message can be just as bad as not telling the truth, when it changes the overall meaning of the message. It doesn't mean that you have to tell employees things that they don't really need to know.

Conversely, however, you must tell them everything that they truly do need to know. When giving instructions, remember:

The "why" is more important than the "I."

GENUINE

Technically speaking, it is possible to be truthful without being genuine. On the other hand, you can never be genuine without being truthful.

Genuine means being sincere, well meaning, and faithful. Genuine refers to your true intention and your honest feelings. Apart from the meaning of being genuine, basic factual accuracy only involves the truthfulness and completeness of the facts and the spoken words themselves, not the spirit behind them.

People instantly recognize sarcasm and ridicule as a lack of sincerity. The necessity for being genuine goes all the way back to our original discussion of self-image.

People with poor self-images tend to be defensive in their communications. They cover up their feelings, and attempt to protect themselves from perceived threats to their position by resorting to deviousness and avoidance.

Genuine leaders don't need to put on an act because they are truly happy serving others. Their written and verbal communications always reflect this sincerity of spirit.

ECONOMICAL

Keep messages as short and to the point as you can. Don't say any more than you need to in order to get your point across. So, how short is short? Who knows? Just long enough to be explicit, simple, sensible, accurate, and genuine.

There is no magic formula to use. If your message is too short, you'll find that out when your listener asks you many questions you haven't fully answered. You can always add more words if you need to, but you can't take one of them back.

Brevity is basic for all communications. Just how brief depends to a great deal on the receiver. If your receiver has no choice in the matter and must read or listen to your message regardless of their desire to do so, then the length only becomes critical if it is so long that it hinders your message's simplicity and sensibility.

However, brevity becomes a much more important factor when your receiver has the choice of tuning you out. You will lose your receiver's attention if your message is long or boring. If you message is too long or too rambling, you'll fail to communicate.

SOCIABLE

Be polite in tone and manner. Your body language and the tone of your voice are just as important and sometimes more meaningful than the actual words that are said.

There is no place for discourtesy and anger in the workplace. People do not usually respond very well to threats and innuendo. They usually become defensive and withdrawn.

A TIMELESS TIP

> **You can catch more bees with honey than you can with vinegar.**

By gosh, that tip seems to be another one of those old saying that just fits this situation perfectly.

Good managers lead others with mutual respect. They don't create fear. A good sense of humor will go a long way in helping you reach a good balance between sociability and firmness.

Well that's it. That's all there is to MESSAGES. Please don't worry about trying to commit all of these tips and tidbits to memory. That's too much to ask.

MESSAGES isn't meant to be a step-by-step set of rules and regulations.

Effective communicating results from a combination of many things. Choosing proper words, using correct grammar, the tone of your voice, your delivery style and body language, your ability to articulate, and even your vocal accent will each have a different affect on your communications effectiveness.

Which of the above factors is the most important for effective communications is open to much discussion. I think it depends on the job you have, and the people you deal with on a routine basis.

Building your vocabulary and learning the proper rules of grammar certainly can't hurt in any circumstance.

The more words you have to choose from, the more capable you will be at selecting words that your listener can understand.

Having a good, practical, useful vocabulary doesn't just mean that you know a lot of big words. The important thing is that you use the right word for the situation.

Don't try to impress someone by talking over their head, using big words they don't understand. The only impression you'll make is a bad one.

Your tone of voice and your body language can add real excitement and emotion to your conversations. Don't be afraid to display lively animation in your speaking.

Remember, managers are human just like everyone else. Don't be aloof and detached from the very workers you are relying on to make you successful.

If you're feeling happy, smile. If you're excited, show your enthusiasm. For firmness, try raising your volume slightly, and lowering the tone of your voice.

Fifty years ago, as an elocution teacher, Kenny's mother tried to teach me to articulate and enunciate exactly the same as everyone else. I think she taught the Standard American pronunciation. She really had a tough job in New Orleans, especially with me.

Sadly, many working people do articulate and enunciate certain words so poorly that they are very difficult to understand.

I've found that these people usually don't have any trouble understanding those same words themselves. When they hear someone else say the word they understand it. They just have a problem when they pronounce the word because they think they are saying it correctly.

Here's a hint for when you're having trouble understanding someone. Correctly repeat the word that you think they are saying. They will understand you when you say the word, and will tell you if you're getting it right. If it isn't the right word, keep repeating similar sounding words until you get the right one.

It's up to you to listen to these people more closely. You'll often need to help them make themselves understood.

In the past, regional vocal accents had much more influence on verbal communications than they do today.

Television news reporting has had a great impact in the area of lessening the one-time stigma of regional accents. On a daily basis, people are now exposed to accents from all over the country, and, for that matter, from all around the entire world.

People have become accustomed to hearing accents from the south, north, east, west, and everywhere in between.

In the end, it's your receivers that will let you know just how well you are communicating. If you don't see or hear the responses that you expected, the problem could be you.

If you are having problems, perhaps reviewing the guidelines for using MESSAGES will help you to better understand why you aren't being understood.

Learning to communicate more effectively is a totally personal proposition. It's really not important for your

131

speaking and writing to fit a rigid common pattern. In fact, even the rules of grammar and punctuation have become much more flexible for modern business usage.

The important thing is that you succeed in getting your ideas across, and that you fully understand what others are trying to tell you. That's it. Nothing more! Nothing less!

Finally, when you're trying to persuade someone to use your ideas, I truly believe that you have to passionately believe in the ideas that you are selling. If you don't have enough self-confidence to believe in your own ideas, why should *I*? Don't waste your time and mine.

A TIMELESS TIP

> **When you want to make your point,**
> **and you want to do it well,**
> **gather all the featured facts,**
> **and sell, sell, sell!**

As we'll see in the following chapters, communications affect each and every aspect of life in the working world. So far, we've talked about real leadership, healthy self-images, and improved communications.

We'll investigate how each of these factors enters into the overall picture of goal setting and planning in the next chapter.

CHAPTER 8

"Dreaming and Scheming"

> **If you don't know where you want to go,
> you'll never know where you are along the way,
> or why you wanted to go in the first place.**

I started learning about heaven and hell when I was in the first grade. Right then and there, I decided that my main goal in life was to make sure I went to heaven.

Don't get me wrong, I'm not preaching hellfire and brimstone. For that matter, I don't know if I even believe in a hell full of fire myself. But, if there is a hell and it's anything like I've heard it's supposed to be, I'm not willing to risk that I might be damned wrong. No pun intended.

Let's face it, when it comes to taking risk, not believing in heaven and hell is the biggest one you'll ever face.

Even though I've been planning to go to heaven for a long time, I certainly don't know for sure if my plans are working. I'll freely admit that I've made several serious detours along the way. I sure hope I'm back on the right road now.

One thing is certain: With every passing day, each of us is steadily getting closer and closer to finding the answer to the greatest mystery of life.

133

So, in the meantime, I figure I might as well be happy and live life to the fullest, and I'll just keep on taking risks, at least until the rotund one sings.

Did you ever stop to think that if old Christopher Columbus didn't have his crazy dream of reaching the east by sailing to the west, he never would have discovered America?

What a risky idea that was. Everybody thought he was going to fall off the edge of the earth. He hatched an ill planned scheme to fulfill his lifelong dream. Captain Chris was one heck of a salesman. Who knew he could line up a rich old Queen to sponsor his three ship sailing team?

Everyone needs to dream dreams. We all need goals to attain. Without goals we have nothing to live for. Our dreams are our goals, and our schemes are the plans we make to achieve them. But, beware; chasing your dreams without having good schemes usually creates nightmares.

In the emotional eulogy that Senator Edward M. Kennedy gave for his brother, Robert F. Kennedy, he stated that Bobby's favorite quote was a play on the words of George Bernard Shaw:

**"Some men see things as they are
and say, Why?
I   dream things that never were and say, Why not?"**

This tribute paid to Bobby Kennedy sums up the essence of our need to create and follow the dreams we have for our lives. Our dreams nurture our imaginations, and provide us with visions and hopes for the future.

Lots of people live by guess and by golly. They set no goals and they make no plans. Then they wonder why they seldom accomplish much of anything. Dreams without schemes aren't really goals at all, they're just fantasies.

Like the usual dialogue between two young lovers trying to decide where to go on a date. "What movie do you want to see?" "I don't know. What movie do you want to see?" I don't know, you decide." Have you ever heard that kind of conversation before?

If you don't know where you want to go, you'll never know where you are along the way, or why you wanted to go in the first place. Above all else, staying in business should be every company's main goal, and that goal can never change if the company is to survive.

Profit

is not a four letter word.

Usually, the only way to stay in business is by making a sufficient profit. Your company isn't a business if it doesn't aim to make a profit. It's a charity. But, even charities need to bring in as much money as they spend or else they won't be around very long either.

The current thinking is that all organizations should develop a Mission Statement. A company then sets its goals in order to carry out its mission. Top management sets overall company goals.

Setting goals and making plans all boils down to one main thing, taking risks. People with positive self-images take reasonable risks. People with low self-esteem take foolish risks or no risk at all. They fear failure and they fear success.

Managers at every level need to set clear goals for themselves and their workers. A manager can't have any guesses about the goals of the company.

Managers must make sure their goals fall in line with the company goals. Running a business is like conducting a symphony; everyone has to be in harmony.

Goals are also called objectives and targets. I place all business goals into two main types:

General and Specific.

General goals tend to remain the same for the life of the company.

**General goals usually dictate company policy,
govern overall operational procedures,
and outline how the company
will be managed.**

Many companies put their general goals in writing, and they give them to all of their employees. They put them on plaques and hang them on walls. They print them in company reports and use them in their advertising.

They think that's all they have to do. Then they promptly fail to makes the necessary plans needed to meet their own goals.

Joe Bonura, Jr., a nationally known sales trainer and inspirational speaker, and my long time friend of over forty years, started his working career with nothing more than an idea and the energy to put his idea in motion.

He set his goal to retire from the advertising agency business before he was fifty. He did exactly that. Joe always makes this point to his audiences during the executive management seminars that he presents:

"Fail to plan and you plan to fail."

I don't think Joe made that proverb up, but whoever did surely deserves lots of credit. It says it like it is.

Specific goals determine the objectives a company must actually accomplish, in order to meet their general goals. Goals come in all shapes and sizes. There are long-term specific, intermediate specific and short-term specific goals.

A company's specific goals tend to change primarily in response to competitive forces in the specific marketplace and with the economy in general.

Long-term specific goals usually set the overall direction a company will take to achieve their wide ranging long-term objectives.

Intermediate goals are usually more specific than long-term goals, and short-term goals are often very specific.

The owner/manager of a small company usually sets all of the company's goals, and normally does all of the planning as well.

In larger companies, most low-level and mid-level managers don't have much voice in setting overall company goals. Previously set budgets, already assigned people, and the available equipment and facilities all restrict the goals that an individual manager can set.

If you find that your goals are constantly changing because they are not being met, either your goals are too high or the level of your real effort is too low.

In 1953, I wanted to become an architect. According to my long-range plan, I enrolled in the Architectural Engineering program at LSU. My long term mission was to create places for people to live and work. By 1954, after I had encountered "Analytic Geometry", my plans suddenly changed.

I must confess that the energy level of my effort to learn Analytics was about as low as my final grade in the course. It was a temporary setback to my plans for becoming the world's best home builder and designer.

When my first plan failed, I simply changed plans. I earned a B.S. in Business Administration instead, and joined the United States Air Force. By 1959 I had become an honest to goodness jet-jockey. At Uncle Sam's insistence, that plan lasted exactly five years, one month, and thirteen days.

Since then my plans have continued to change as life unfolded. I've worked in numerous widely differing fields.

I've worked in food and beverage container manufacturing, real estate sales and management, meat processing, building and off-shore construction, carpet sales, asphalt refining, shell dredging, steel fabrication, electric sign manufacture, bulk abrasives manufacturing, heavy weight aggregate sales, professional speaking, consulting, and college teaching.

I have also been a consultant to other talented people engaged in plumbing, general contracting, cosmetology, retail food service, advertising, demolition, and professional entertainment.

As things turned out, almost forty years after self-destructing in LSU's School of Architectural Engineering, I actually have provided many places for people to work and live.

My most enjoyable building activity has been doing the technical consulting for a number of renovation and remodeling projects for non-profit groups.

Their goals are to improve the housing conditions affecting disadvantaged people living in our decaying inner-cities.

In 1992, I learned that re-creating old things was a much greater challenge than creating new things. That's when some friends and I organized a new non-profit corporation, dedicated to rebuilding blighted neighborhoods in the inner-cities of America. The organization is called CAPRA (The Community and People's Recovery Association).

Obviously, between 1953 and 1994, my career plans changed direction more times than the Mississippi River.

However, it appears that my overall goal of creating things has never changed. Somehow, I think "Analytics" wasn't really a mountain after all; it was only a mole hill.

Do Street Smart Managers always meet every goal they set? No way! Anyone who claims that they always meet their goals is probably not aiming very high to begin with.

Can you still be happy when you don't meet all of your goals? Absolutely! The real fun is in the trying.

President John F. Kennedy's goal was to land a man on the moon. Kennedy set the goal and NASA had to figure out how to make it happen. NASA had to make plans to do things that nobody had ever done before, and they carried them out.

NASA people aren't all that special. They're ordinary folks, just like you and me. But, in truth, there is one crucial difference between NASA people and most of us. We don't have a rich uncle who prints his own money.

**Specific goals tell you the steps
you specifically need to accomplish
in order to get a specific job done.**

In other words, everyone in a company has a certain job to do, and it's up to you to get yours done. Street Smart Managers realize that reaching the company's goals is the best way of meeting their on individual dreams and goals.

When a company succeeds, everyone working for that company succeeds. When a company fails, everyone suffers along with it. Your goals and your company's goals must always be compatible.

Goals must be based on sound decisions, not on guesses. Goals need to be clear, not cloudy. Goals range from simple goals that are easy to accomplish, all the way to highly ambitious and far reaching goals. Great goals call for great expectations. Goals have to come first, then plans. You can't have one without the other.

Street Smart Managers make sure that they understand the company goals before they set their own individual departmental goals.

A TIMELESS TIP

> **Stick with facts
> not fantasies.**

Once your goals have been identified, the next step is planning. Any ordinary person with an average intelligence and a healthy self-image can be a good planner, simply by using normal common sense in order to meet common goals.

People tend to think of planning as some academic and highly scientific process that requires years of study and files of research. Nothing could be further from the truth. Surely, planners do need to have certain types of scientific information and accurate research data available. That's why God invented scientists and researchers.

A TIMELESS TIP

> **Facts and figures change good figuring doesn't.**

There are plenty of textbooks outlining long lists of different methods of planning and types of plans being used in all sorts of situations.

Here's a partial list of plans you can pick and choose from:

Strategic Plans
Operational Plans
Specific Plans
Directional Plans
Functional Plans
Development Plans
Short-term Plans

Long-term Plans
One-time Plans
Program Plans
Standing Plans
Standby Plans
Emergency Plans

Get the picture? There's a kind of plan for anything you can possibly dream up.

At this point, I'm not concerned with the technical differences between all of these types of plans.

Don't worry about those minor differences, once you know the fundamentals, you can plan anything. Street Smart Managers practice planning at the street level.

The same fundamentals apply no matter what type of plan you are developing. Planning is an innate human undertaking that always involves the same six basic activities. We'll cover those in the next chapter.

Planning is just like good Creole cooking. A great gumbo always starts with the same ingredients: Onions, celery, bell peppers, a little garlic, and a smooth brown roux.

The time tested method, used by all good planners, combines clear goals with sufficient facts, lots of logic, some good old well seasoned intuition, adequate resources, and plenty of leadership and action.

That's the recipe. When you understand the basics, the fine art of planning comes naturally. When you're willing to take the heat in the kitchen, you usually get a good share of the dessert.

All of life takes planning and some people do plan better than others.

However, the fact remains that everyone must make plans constantly. What to eat? What to wear? Just getting to work takes planning. How many people do you know that can't even plan well enough to get to work on time?

This brings up an important point about implementing plans. It takes leadership to make plans work. Unfortunately, not all people have the leadership ability to lead others.

People who can't even carry out the little plans designed to meet little goals, certainly can't be expected to execute big plans needed for reaching big goals.

Street Smart Managers use the practical approach when planning to meet their goals. Planning is a cumulative activity.

Successfully planning and meeting lots of small goals usually evolves into successfully planning and meeting bigger goals.

Even if you own a one-person business, planning is still a cooperative activity. Don't forget to consider others, such as: your customers, your banker, your suppliers, and your CPA.

Successful planning doesn't take place in a vacuum. Effective planning takes a lot of looking, listening, and thinking.

Look around to see what you're up against. What you see will give you lots of insights into the people and things you'll be working with.

That's the reason why "shirt-sleeve" managers are always out and about their work areas. They know the importance of visual contact.

As planned activities begin to unfold, good working plans call for all activities to appear as they normally should, so always watch out for things that appear unusual. First impressions can be extremely valuable indicators of many unseen management troubles in a business. That's why every time I've ever taken on a new management troubleshooting assignment, the very first thing I did was make a quick walk-around. I just wanted to see how things looked.

I looked at the variations in different people's levels of activity. I observed their moods and facial expressions.

Simply watching people at their normal work stations can tell you volumes. I also took a close look at the things that the people were using.

The amount of time, energy, money, and care devoted to housekeeping and maintenance generally tells a lot about a company's planning and priorities.

Dirty housekeeping and poor maintenance are sure signs of big problems somewhere. Either there's not enough money to do things right, or the people in charge don't really care. When looking around, remember this: What you see is what you get.

Listening to the people you'll be working with is one of the best risk reducers you can find. Unless you know everything there is to know, always get as many facts and opinions as you can before you plan.

You don't have to believe what everyone tells you and you don't have to accept every opinion you are given. However, you'll usually end up with most of the real facts and some sound opinions if you take the time and effort to listen to the people.

A TIMELESS TIP

> **It's better to listen
> to an idea you don't choose
> than to overlook
> the best idea you could have used.**

It takes self-confidence to set imaginative goals, and to have the faith that you can reach them. It takes authority and responsibility to turn those goals from ideas into reality. It takes good communication skills to gather the information needed for making plans, and for convincing others that your plans will work.

We've looked at why dreams are important, and why the process of planning is crucial to turning your dreams into realities. In the next chapter we'll take a closer look at the fundamentals of the processes of planning and problem solving.

CHAPTER 9

"First Things First"

Time – Money - People - Things

As a manager, I've always tried to get as many of my employees involved in the strategic planning process as I could. I firmly believe that the more people you have giving you advice the better. Having said that, I have always followed one hard and fast rule without exception. In a nutshell, it goes like this:

Whenever I ask for an opinion about a possible plan of action, I definitely want to be told when anyone thinks it is going to fail. Good workable plans should create positive "gut feelings" in everyone that's involved. If you don't have confidence in a plan, say so! You may very well be right.

If I go ahead with a plan that someone said he or she thought would fail, and it actually does fail; then it's my entire problem. I'm always willing to listen to someone tell me: "I told you so." Luckily, that hasn't happened to me very often. However, I never, ever, want to hear anyone tell me, "I could have told you so."

If that person could have told me so, I think that person should have told me so. In my mind, that kind of "YES" person is not reliable. There's no excuse for not speaking your mind when you have the chance.

Now, for some specific ideas about planning. Here's the normal sequence for the six basic planning activities of a Street Smart Manager:

1) **Determine the exact job at hand.**
2) **Gather all the facts and figures.**
3) **Consider alternatives and risks.**
4) **Choose an alternative.**
5) **Try it and give it time.**
6) **Make changes as needed.**

For general planning purposes, specific goals and task descriptions amount to the same thing. The first step in planning is to analyze the exact task at hand. All plans must be based on fact, not fantasy.

Quite often, the first thing you'll have to do is to question the timing of goal that somebody else gives you to reach. All too often, there isn't enough planning time to do adequate research and planning for the job.

One of the most frequently seen examples of setting unrealistic goals is when not enough time is allowed for getting a complex job completed. This is particularly true in industries such as building construction and specialty manufacturing.

A TIMELESS TIP

It's better to not try what seems improbable, than to prove it was impossible.

Judging whether a goal is reachable requires determining as accurately as possible the full requirements and specifications for the project. If your assigned job has not been made clear, be sure to get it cleared up before you go any further. A misunderstanding that might seem insignificant at the beginning could be become critical at the end. It's impossible to do a good job of planning if you don't do a good job of finding out exactly what you have to plan.

This story about the time a tame Tiger had a wild job by the tail is a true-life example of a very costly misunderstanding. It was the result of not knowing the full requirements of a job at hand.

Shortly after I had taken on the risky job of reorganizing a troubled steel fabrication firm, I found out that one of the largest projects under construction was for the NASA space program.

The job called for constructing a huge steel pipe structure called a "load cell." It was going to be used to support a NASA space shuttle booster-tank during the manufacture of the tanks.

It was fabricated of large, heavy, round "T-1" steel pipe, and was at least twenty feet wide by twenty feet high. When it was finished it was so large that it had to be shipped to the NASA plant by a river barge.

The job was contracted before I had gone to work for the company, and it was being completed when I arrived on the scene. As is normal with most government jobs, the company had been awarded the job because they had submitted the lowest bid. Unfortunately, the bid was way too low.

When our company bid the job, nobody in either the estimating or production departments were aware that there was a major difference between the welding procedures for "T-1" steel and "Mild" steel. To make things worse, after the structure was shipped, it was rejected because all of the pipe welds failed NASA's performance tests.

Up until that time, all of the other structures they had fabricated had been made using "Mild" steel. It was a little to too late when they learned that the difference wasn't just in the name.

"T-1" steel must be preheated and then post-heated while it is being welded. "Mild" steel required neither of these two very costly special treatments.

Not only didn't our estimators allow for the extra labor and the added expenses of preheating and post-heating, the engineering department didn't even tell the welders that they had to preheat and post-heat each of the welds.

That's where Tiger came in. He was our best fitter/welder, and a super-duper diplomat. His given name was Francis, but we all called him Tiger.

150

Since the load cell was already on site at NASA's location and the shuttle tank project that it was to be used for was way behind schedule, it was impractical to bring it back to our fabrication yard, so we sent Tiger to it.

Tiger spent nearly two months cutting apart and re-welding every single welded joint on the load cell. Tiger was at the customer's site for so long that everybody over there thought he was on NASA's payroll. We sure wished that he was, but there was no such luck for us.

Our planners missed their costs projection on that job by the proverbial mile. Their (I)s might have been dotted, but they certainly didn't make sure that all of their (T)s were crossed.

Once your job expectations are completely understood, then it's a matter of gathering data and systematically determining the resources needed to accomplish the job.

No matter what your objective is, planning for it will require looking at pertinent facts, figures, and opinions, and that calls for gathering information. If your job is to meet a certain sales goal, you'll need accurate information about the potential market for your product.

If your job is to find a new product for your company to make and sell, you'll need to find out what special needs people have that your company might meet. This takes research.

In other words, different planning jobs require different information, but you still need to gather the pertinent facts and figures.

You will also need to judge the completeness and accuracy of the facts and figures that you gather. You may often need to rely on help from outside scientist and researchers to provide you with information you don't have.

Hopefully, the overall planning picture is starting to come into focus. But remember, if you start with fuzzy facts and figures, you'll never get a clear picture. Planning takes a combination of common sense, intuition, vision, and faith.

Planning variables can be placed in four basic areas of consideration:

Time,
Money,
People, and
Things

These fabulous four resources not only affect each other, they also affect every other essential factor that is in any way involved with planning. Consider them the "kissing cousins" of effective planning. For brevity, I refer to them as the **TMPT** functions of planning.

These four sides make up the basic framework of planning. All four parts have an impact on the final picture. I call it painting the planning portrait. Just like a good photograph, everything has to be in focus.

The first thing to ask is "How much time do I have?" If there's not enough time, nothing else matters.

Time governs everything.

It's hard for me to conceive of any business activity being accomplished efficiently and effectively when the original time line for completion doesn't allow for proper planning time before the job is started.

Time affects money, people, and things in an adverse order. The less time you have the more of everything else you will need.

A TIMELESS TIP

> **If you can't find time**
>
> **to plan the first time,**
>
> **where will you find the time**
> **to plan the job over again?**

Next comes Money. Do you have the financial means to complete the job, given the time and the people assigned, and the things available? Many people go broke because they started a job they couldn't afford to finish.

The amount of money you need is definitely affected by the time you have. Short-term jobs may incur excessive cost because you have to hire extra people, and/or buy or lease more equipment in order to meet the deadline. Long-term jobs might be a financial burden because of cash-flow problems, caused by customers who delay payments for the work already done. Long-term jobs generally incur extra interest expense.

When it comes to the effects of time on the need for money, there is no rule of thumb. Each case must stand on its own.

The third side of the planning square is People. Do you have the right workers? Do you have enough workers? Again, planning for the number of people needed for a job is a function related to the other three: Time, Money, and Things.

Within limitations, the less time you have, the more people you'll need. If it takes two people to complete a job in two days, then four workers could be probably complete the same job in one day. That is assuming they wouldn't be getting in each other's way.

If you're not paying a premium price, use as many people as you can effectively use to complete your jobs as quickly as possible. When there are no time constraints, then money considerations would likely dictate using as few people as possible to finish the job efficiently.

There are usually a definable minimum number of people needed to accomplish every job efficiently. Most plans call for using no more than the minimum number of people needed for the job at hand.

For example, the fact that one person can't physically be at both ends of a long board of lumber at one time creates a situation where two people are needed to nail up such a board.

Using less people over a longer time will usually result in a lower labor cost. However, it's generally better to be waiting around for another opportunity to come along, than to lose precious opportunities because you aren't ever ready for them as they come.

No matter what type of work you do, time is the only thing you can't replace. You can hire new people to replace people that leave. You can raise more money, and you can buy or lease more equipment; but you can never replace lost time.

On the other hand, it's not good to overload a work area. There's an old New Orleans proverb: "Too many cooks spoil the Creole cream cheese."

Finally, don't plan to pay overtime on a permanent basis. Overtime should be a short-term solution to a temporary problem. Deciding if the available people have the right talents depends on the requirements of the job.

Having talent doesn't just mean having job knowledge. It also includes having the ability to use that knowledge, having the capacity to work with others, and having the self-motivation to use that talent to the fullest.

The specific knowledge needed to perform any given job successfully is generally directly related to the amount of supervision that will be available on the job.

155

People who work with little or no supervision need to have an extensive knowledge about the work they're doing. Line-supervisors need to know more than line-workers. Mid-level managers need to have more knowledge than line-supervisors. Top-level managers should have a complete mastery of their particular areas of expertise.

Considering the *Things* that are needed is the final step in completing the four-sided planning portrait. Do you have the right equipment? Certain jobs can't be done efficiently unless the workers have the right equipment.

Poor equipment maintenance is a serious problem in many companies. Having equipment that doesn't work on a job is just as bad as not having it to on the job to begin with.

Many companies start out with sufficient equipment, but they fail to keep up with the latest technological advances, and they end up with old, obsolete, inefficient, costly, and non-competitive equipment.

Obsolescence is not just a small company problem. Look at what happened to the primary steel industry in the United States.

Computers are neat, they add and subtract really, really, really fast. But, computers can't solve your management problems, and they can't make your decisions for you. Computers aren't like TV sets. You don't just turn one on and wait for it to entertain you. Many times computers cause more problems than they solve.

Computers are great at eliminating repetitive tasks, keeping voluminous records, retrieving stored information, and printing out reams and reams of reports.

We live in the information age, with computers, satellites, faxes, and e-mails. You name it! We've got it! Interpreting and using the information you gather is another matter.

People spend huge amounts of time entering useless data into computers, and print out report after report. Reports that few people read, and even fewer people understand.

A TIMELESS TIP

> **Reports are often a day late
> and a dollar short.**

There's really no reason in today's Internet world for anyone to come up short on finding out extensive information about almost anything.

There's another old saying I've heard time and time again.

"Figures don't lie, but liars figure."

Always check out your sources. Sometimes a few statistical calculations can make the difference between success and failure.

Statisticians support planners, and many large companies have statisticians on their staff. If you don't have a statistician on your staff, check out your nearest university.

Many universities have set up a small business department that will work with you. They can help you find the precise business expertise you need.

After you have gathered all of the data that you think you need, the next step is to develop one or more plans of action that you believe will accomplish the task at hand.

You may feel that one plan is so workable that it is the only one you need to consider.

Developing only one plan is quite common when owner/managers plan projects that are routine and ordinary for their business. However, several alternatives are usually developed when a job is complicated or involves operations that are not routine.

Alternatives will vary according to the means you have at your disposal, and subject to the methods of management that you chose.

As I said before, all undertakings involve:

Time, Money, People, and Things

Your company's flexibility in these four basic planning variables will determine how many practical alternatives you'll have for any given project.

The more choices you have to choose from, the better are your chances of being successful. For example, Alternative (A) might take more time than money. Alternative (B) might call for more money than time.

On the practical side, most companies have limited planning time and resources to devote to trying to exhaust every possible alternative for any given problem.

Be practical! I know people who can't stop planning. They keep trying to make their plans perfect, and they never get around to really doing anything.

Most of your plans are likely to be plans for things that you are pretty sure you can achieve. In planning, the first set of considerations deals with:

Possibility vs. Probability

Each plan should first be evaluated to determine if overall goal of the plan is actually possible, and then each and every part of the plan must actually be possible to accomplish. It's important to remember that advances in technology constantly change the possibility that certain things can be accomplished.

Not that long ago in the history of man, it wasn't possible for humans to live over 100,000 feet above the earth's surface. Then we learned to orbit the earth. Not many years later man walked on the moon. Within the next twenty-years, we could fly out to orbit and back to earth again. For centuries, we couldn't see very clearly beyond the atmosphere. Then came along the Hubbell Space Telescope.

Time changes almost everything, but we still can't fool Mother Nature, keep it from raining on our parade, or cure the common cold.

A TIMELESS TIP

> **There is a very big distinction between the possibility that something can be done and the probability that you can actually do it.**

Sometimes, some of the variations in the alternate plans won't really have any effect on the overall outcome of each plan.

Modern statistical analysis might help tell you which variables have no effect on any particular plan.

Having all the facts and figures, coming up with alternatives, and carefully evaluating each plan is necessary. Nevertheless, sooner or later, you'll have to decide what you're going to do.

The second set of guidelines is based on the rules of:

Reason and Reality

Reason requires you to consider the logic of each of your alternatives.

Does one plan make more sense than the other plan? Which plan has more contingencies? Does each plan flow in an orderly manner? Vague and disorderly plans usually run into trouble.

Reality calls for an honest assessment of your practical ability to carry out each plan. Do you really have the time? Do you really have the money? Do you really have the people and the things you need?

A plan may look good on paper, but even if there is just one part of it that you really can't carry out, then the plan probably won't work. Don't try to fool yourself by thinking you can do the impossible. The only fool will be you.

The third standard for making a choice is perhaps the most important by far. Ask yourself this simple question about each plan:

If this plan fails,
can I live with the worst possible outcome?

161

Discard every plan that doesn't generate a "Yes" answer to that question! Then compare the various expected outcomes and risks of each of the remaining plans.

The fourth and fifth steps in planning are:

Deciding and Doing

Lots of people don't make final decisions because they don't want to fail. Planning overkill is an easy trap to fall into. These kinds of people usually suffer from very low self-esteem.

When people fail to make a decision, they are really deciding that they'll just accept the status quo. They say: "Whatever happens happens!" They let life run them, instead of them running their lives.

The only reason managers get paid more than their subordinates, is because managers must make more decisions. As managers get paid more, the decisions they have to make normally become more and more critical to the overall welfare of the company.

Managers and owners who can't make timely decisions eventually lose their jobs, or they go out of business. Business problems don't go away on their own. They just get worse.

"If it ain't broke, don't fix it." That's good advice up to a point. But, if you never try something new you may never know what improvements can be made.

Pick a plan and do it! Put everything in motion and see what happens. Each part of a plan should be important. If any step in the plan isn't important, it shouldn't be in the plan to begin with.

Many plans don't work out; simply because they get stopped, before they really get started. The planner loses faith in the plan. They get "buyer's remorse." Unless you encounter serious problems, don't stop a plan prematurely. Nothing humans do is perfect, and nothing we will do is ever going to be perfect.

Choose the plan that makes the most sense, and has the best chance of being carried out; with the least risk of Time, Money, People, and Things.

"If you're going to do something, do it right!" The first person who said that was one smart cookie. Doing it right calls for giving a plan enough time to work out. Good Cajun cooks put the pot on the fire, and let the crackling fry till it's sweet and tasty. We call it Cajun Candy. But I must admit, nothing taste worse than half cooked pig fat. Let your plans cook, through and through.

The final set of standards addresses the continuing nature of the whole planning and problem solving process:

Checking and Changing

Checking out how a plan is progressing is a matter of following a planned timetable, and determining pre-set criteria for gauging the results as the plan progresses. Your criteria should include testing all of the expected results, in all of the four basic planning areas.

Are things happening within the time planned? Are the costs within the budget? How much labor has been expended, as compared to the estimated cost of labor? Are the systems and the equipment doing the job they were supposed to do?

There's usually a learning curve involved in doing anything for the first time.

Results might well improve dramatically over a short period-of-time, so give your plan enough time to allow for the improvements to take place. After you've taken enough time to check your plan thoroughly, then it's time to make changes needed to improve the results.

While it is important not to make changes prematurely, it's also imperative to make changes as soon as you have no doubt that certain changes are needed.

Planning is a process of continual creativity, and it requires a clear vision of growth and progress. Exactly when planning stops and problem solving starts is an intriguing question, though I don't think it's worth much effort worrying about it.

In daily business operations, planning and problem solving can be viewed as the same thing. The steps involved are identical. However, most people only think of problems as things that go wrong. Problems are not always bad. Problems resulting from success are generally good problems.

Either way you look at it, you can't escape the fact that planning and problem solving are an integral part of daily life, personally and in your business life.

A TIMELESS TIP

Planning takes time.
Take the time to plan.
It pays off.

To review, Street Smart Managers use the following universal set of procedures and guidelines for choosing alternatives:

1) The initial step deals with the gauging the actual potential of the various plans.
2) The second addresses the operation of the plans.
3) The third compares the outcomes and relative risks of each plan.
4) The fourth governs decisions.
5) The fifth covers the implementation.
6) The sixth phase covers evaluation and change.

The next chapter explores the fine art of finding a successful solution to fit each problem you face.

CHAPTER 10

"Sunrise"

> **The only certain thing in life is uncertainty.**
> **Be prepared for change.**

I called this chapter "Sunrise" because every sunrise brings a new day, and with every new day there are new possibilities. With every new problem there are new challenges and endless new opportunities.

Nothing in the physical world ever stays the same. Babies are born and people die. Today's young people are tomorrow's old folks. Nature builds and nature destroys. Time moves on, without missing a beat. As the words of the popular song say: "Everything old is new again."

Uncertainty is truly the only certain thing in life. The end of the world comes for somebody every day.

The only thing that I've found that remains the same is the nature of the human spirit. We still have all our needs, wants, and faults. Our human spirit gives us the insight to admit we have faults, and gives us the drive to overcome them.

People with a healthy self-image take a positive approach, and they face their problems straight on.

Pessimists lack self-confidence, and they turn away from their problems hoping they'll go away. Problems don't go away, they just change appearances.

Every problem in the world can be traced to humanity's efforts to meet our basic needs, and to the drive to satisfy our ever growing list of wants. Solving problems brings progress, and progress brings more problems.

A TIMELESS TIP

> **Be prepared for change
> and never say never!**

Life is a swinging pendulum, moving back and forth between progress and problems. I call this endless process the **Success /Problem Cycle**.

As I've pointed out in the previous chapter, problem solving and planning are essentially similar tasks. Now I'll combine the two operations together, and classify both of these activities under one master heading that encompasses the most important function of all managers:

Decision Making

In the knock-down, drag-out world of business, making good decisions separates the winners from the losers.

Making plans and solving problems involves all of the steps we discussed before, but the nitty-gritty bottom line is this:

It's your decisions that count.

There is no set formula for making good decisions. Flexibility is the key to solving most problems. Rigidity usually causes problems. It doesn't solve them.

The best suggestions I have for dealing with the stress of handling most problems are: "Hang loose." "Take'em as they come." "Roll with the punches."

I believe that the ideas in this chapter are as valid for the one-person shop as well as for the largest corporation. However, for simplicity's sake, this chapter is slanted towards managers with wide ranging responsibilities.

Anybody who says, "It's lonely at the top", is evidently doing something wrong. No one can survive alone at the top.

Making good decisions requires help from everyone. It has to be a team effort. Even people who run one-person operations have to consider their customers and their supplies in all of their decisions.

Don't try to solve your problems all alone. Heed the words in this popular song: "You'll get by with a little help from your friends."

Everybody has problems and everyone makes mistakes. I don't care how rich you are, how powerful you are, or how smart you are; everybody has problems.

Show me a person without any problems and I show you a person without a life. At the least, I'll show you a person with very little ambition.

As a matter of fact, according to my theory of the Success/Problem Cycle; the more success you have, the more problems you'll have. Think about it. People go into business expecting to make money. If it's your business, you want to be successful.

To be successful, your business needs to keep growing. When you increase sales, you'll need to make more products. That's a good problem!

When you succeed with making more products, you'll need more storage space. Another good problem. When you solve the storage problem, you'll have more inventory; then you'll need to sell more product. The cycle just keeps on going, and going, and going.

Consider the example of my friend Leon, the plumber. After Leon finished school, he got a job as a plumber's helper, working for a large mechanical contractor.

Leon has a really sharp mind, and he's a hard worker. In a very short period of time he learned the trade and reached the rank of master plumber.

When he reached the master plumber stage, he faced another good problem. He was at the top wage scale in the company and he wanted to make more money. So he decided he would solve that problem by going into business on his own.

He opened his own plumbing business, which, of course, created more problems. Now, instead of being just a master plumber, he was in the plumbing business. There is quite a difference between the two career positions.

Like most other small business operators, Leon started off doing everything himself, and worked the business out of his house. He did the selling. He did the plumbing work. He even tried to keep the books.

Leon was typical of most people who start a service business for themselves.

Being a smart and dedicated worker, with a great natural sales personality, he soon started getting more business than he could handle by himself. That caused him to have another good problem. He needed a good plumber's helper. After he hired a helper, he then had supervision problems.

With his business growing, he needed help with the paperwork. His wife took over that chore. More sales meant that he needed to hire additional plumbers, then more helpers for those plumbers. Then he needed more capital for buying additional trucks and equipment. Soon he had to rent a building because he could no longer work out of his garage. More problems!

The more successful he was, the more good problems he had. Was Leon afraid of facing his problems? No way! Leon has a positive self-image, and he faces his problems one day at a time.

Leon has a developed great reputation with his many customers.

Leon now owns his own commercial building, employs a whole bunch of plumbers and helpers, and has a full staff of people working in the office. Leon has created lots of jobs.

In my book, Leon is a true winner. I guess that's why I put him in my book. Sure he has problems, and he has made his share of mistakes. But he succeeds because he does more things right than wrong and he keeps on solving his problems as they come up.

I'm happy to report that he's still causing problems today.

Making mistakes is not the cause of failure,
failing to learn
from the mistakes you make
is the cause of failure.

I love solving problems. Problems present new challenges and meeting challenges is where the fun is.

Besides, if companies didn't have problems, they wouldn't need good managers.

I'll even go one step further and say this about would-be managers: If you're not spending most of your time working out problems, you are not doing much managing.

The more successful you are the more problems you will surely have. On the bright side, the more successful you are the more resources you'll be gaining, and resources help you solve your problems.

Success is not best determined by how many problems you have to handle, it is better determined by how you handle the problems you have.

As you climb higher up the management ladder, you'll find that you'll have more crucial problems to solve.

Whether you're making initial plans, trying to avoid future problems, or trying to correct a problem that has already occurred, the same basic approach holds true for all cases.

Because you'll need to know how to recognize problems before you can solve them. The rest of this chapter will be devoted to looking at a few techniques for finding and handling problems.

"An ounce of prevention is worth a pound of cure."

One of the most effective things you can do is to recognize a problem before it happens.

I hate to admit it; nevertheless, the Air Force is absolutely right, pilot error is actually the cause of almost all military aircraft accidents.

During the entire five years that I was an Air Force pilot, and in all the years since then, I believe that every single plane crash that I've read about was either directly or indirectly caused by pilot error. Of course, that is with the exception of airplanes that are blown apart by terrorist's bombs.

So what meaning does this example of accident responsibility have for you as a business manager?

It simply dictates that most of your management problems will be caused by the people you supervise, not by the things they use.

No matter what business you're in, it's people who create most of management's problems. With that in mind, let's look at some of the behavioral warning signs that you can easily observe.

Analyzing Early Signs

The Three (A)s will give you advanced warning of problems to come.

The first (A) is for the **attitudes** of the people working with you. Do your workers have good or bad attitudes? Do they come to work on time? Do they cooperate with each other? Are they loyal to the company? Do they generally go the extra distance when needed?

Occasionally, someone with a temporarily bad attitude does make a change.

However, the change is usually because some problem in their personal life has been eliminated or greatly abated.

Domestic, financial, health, and legal problems can all have a temporary or permanent affect on the way people behave at work.

Alcoholism and drug abuse are two serious personal problems that adversely affect millions of workers. Sadly, unless your job description also includes being a social worker, if you try to solve these kinds of destructive personal problems for your workers the probability is very high that sooner or later you'll be faced with serious problems you can't handle.

Don't waste valuable time trying to change a person who has a chronic case of bad attitude. To put it bluntly, bad actors have to go.

Conversely, a boss with poor management technique can certainly cause a normally good employee to behave badly. When confronted by a negative manager, many good employees back away from the situation

Workers view a negative manager with fear and mistrust. They put up defenses against management in general and they tend to hold their own natural self-motivation in check.

The second (A) concerns **adaptability**. Adaptability refers to those personality traits which help someone to roll with the punches. Adaptability allows people to change with a changing world.

Adaptability questions include: Can your workers face changes on the job? Can they handle things that go wrong? Can they do things differently? Can they learn new things? Are they flexible? Technology changes constantly, at an ever increasing rate, and people are being forced to change jobs more frequently.

Jobs that remain the same forever are few and far between.

Problems often arise because people can't or just won't accept certain new people coming into their work group.

Just a few short years ago, I delivered telegrams by hand and rode my bicycle all over town handing out those familiar yellow sheets of paper. How many Western Union boys do you see riding bikes on the streets today?

The litany of changes never comes to an end. Not being able to adapt doesn't make someone a bad person.

Some people really try hard to learn something new, but they just can't adapt to new company policies, or to new methods of production. It's unfortunate, but, unless you can place such a person in a position that doesn't require very much adaptability, you're going to have an overall efficiency problem with that person.

The third (A) is for **activities**. Employees who appear to be mentally distracted from their work will often signal problems ahead.

Observing your employees during their routine work activity can provide you with a multitude of valuable information.

Is your worker doing things any differently than he or she normally does them?

Are some workers doing things that are causing problems with others? Is a worker making more mistakes than normal? Is an employee making simple mistakes that they shouldn't be making at all? Are they too slow, or are they working too fast and producing poor quality results?

Sometimes, good employees do bad things without realizing it. Otherwise good employees can unwittingly engage in activities that are disruptive. Usually, a little on-the-job re-training is all that is needed to correct unintended problematic behavior.

A TIMELESS TIP

> **Good workers
> learn bad habits
> from bad workers.**

People can make you or break you. It only takes one disruptive person to cause serious problems within an entire group. Remember this:

"One bad apple, spoils the barrel."

Wow! Another "Oldie but Goodie." It's amazing how many of these old sayings just keep on going strong. I'll bet someone could write a whole book using nothing but these wise old sayings. Gee! I guess I already did.

Building Your Facts

Whenever any kind of problem comes up unexpectedly, studying these critical factors will help you find out why it happened. Think (B), for "because." This investigative phase will give you the answers that will help complete this important sentence:

"We had the problem because."

The first (B) is for **body count**.

Was there a problem because there were not enough people, or was the problem caused by having the wrong people on the job? Either situation invariably causes a problem. Did the people on the job have the right attitude? Were they adaptable? Were their activities inadequate for the situation? Simply assigning warm bodies to a job isn't the answer to a problem. It causes most of them.

As we discussed previously, there is a definable minimum and maximum number of people that efficiently fit within the scope of any given job. Assigning too few people can be as bad as using too many people.

Common sense and past experience are the best indicators of the numbers of people that can be used efficiently on any given job. Over the long run, trial and error usually provides workable answers.

The second (B) is for **brain power**. Was the problem caused because the people didn't know and understand the things they needed to know in order to complete the plan?

If they didn't know what to do, was it because they were not capable of learning, or was it because nobody taught them what they needed to know? Was there a basic hiring problem, or was there some type of employee training problem?

Management bears the responsibility for making sure that the people assigned to a job know exactly what they need to know. A person who doesn't know and understand what they need to know can't be expected to perform effectively. They certainly can't teach themselves things that they don't know.

The third (B) is for **building blocks**. Was there a problem because you didn't have the right equipment and supplies?

Was the equipment inadequate from the start? Was the equipment not working properly? Were there enough supplies? Did someone order the wrong materials?

There's no denying that not having enough things, having the wrong things, and/or trying to use broken things can certainly cause costly problems.

On the surface, all of these kinds of mechanical problems appear to be related solely to the inanimate things we work with. But this is not so!

The real root problem lies with the person or persons responsible for making sure that the right things were on the job, at the right time, and in good working order. No matter which way you cut it, you'll always find people at the core of every problem, human or mechanical.

Connections

The next group of management's concerns deal with what I call: Personal Connections. Whenever two or more persons are working together, there are certain mental connections that must take place.

The first (C) is for **commitment**. Are your workers committed to the company, to their supervisors, to their peers, to themselves, and to the job at hand? Is there a morale problem within the company? You must have positive dynamics for any group to work harmoniously. Distrust is contagious.

People aren't committed to people they don't respect. Is your boss the cause of the problem? Are you the cause of the problem? If the problem is with your higher management, what can you do about it? Think about that sticky situation for a while.

Workers must be committed to each other. That's not to say that they have to be best friends away from the job. Non-work-place social relationships are for the most part irrelevant to the job. Nevertheless, when on the job, people have to back each other up in every way. Every problem affecting dedication and loyalty must be found and corrected immediately.

A TIMELESS TIP

> **A house divided**
> **cannot stand.**

The second (C) is for **conditions**. Was there a problem with the working conditions?

Was there too little time? Was there too little space? Was there too much sun, too much rain, too much cold, or too much heat? Was there too much lost time?

In a majority of cases, there isn't much chance for human control over natural conditions which affect an outdoor job. Look at what rain and cold can do to a planned space shuttle launch.

Making adequate allowances for weather contingencies is a very important factor in avoiding problems later.

The third (C) is for **competition**. Was there too much competition within your group of workers? Too much internal competition causes friction, too little compatibility causes lethargy. How is the esprit de corps?

Deterrents

Finally, the three (D)s involve deterrents. Deterrents are external obstacles that block the successful completion of a task.

For our purposes, deterrents are factors from outside of the work force itself. In other words, I consider deterrents to be any factor that either the immediate supervisor or the workers have no control over.

Recognizing the deterrents is critical for determining alternate courses of action that might solve your problems.

The first (D) is for **design.** Was the project doomed from the start? Was it simply a bad design or plan of action? No matter how hard people try, they usually can't overcome the problems that result from a plan that is fatally flawed from the start. Not for all the oil in the Arabian desert.

After spending more than thirty years in the real estate maintenance trade, I can tell you that many buildings are designed with serious built-in maintenance problems just waiting to happen. I guess I shouldn't complain, because I've made lots of money fixing architect's mistakes.

The second (D) is for **distractions**. I classify a distraction as anything beyond your personal control. Was there anything that distracted the workers from accomplishing the job? Did anyone or anything interfere with the job? Were the workers called away before the job was finished?

One of the most common incidences is when someone with higher authority pulls people off of one unfinished job to go work on another job.

People enjoy a feeling of accomplishment when they reach their goals. Workers get a feeling of contentment and satisfaction when they see a job reach its completion. This feeling of satisfaction doesn't come about when they are pulled away before the job is done.

The third (D) is for **direction.** Inadequate communications is probably the most common and most serious cause of management problems.

Was there a problem with the instructions given beforehand? Was there a lack of supervision on the job? Many problems result from of a lack of clear understanding between the one initiating the activity and the persons carrying out the activity.

It's very hard, if not impossible, to do something right when you really don't understand exactly what you're supposed to do. I know I've expressed that thought before, but if I repeat it ten more times it won't be too many.

Most operational problems are deeply rooted in troubles within management itself, and the effectiveness of the supervision rendered while a job is in progress is another major concern.

In summary, I've found that using this natural sequence of information gathering for problem solving and planning also helps me to see certain potential problems in advance. However, not all business problems can be eliminated by better planning. There will be those problems that you simply cannot anticipate, and that you cannot control.

Unfortunately, in spite of the fact that there will always be problems that are unforeseen and unavoidable, it remains absolutely true that the responsibility for the success or failure of all business activities falls squarely on the shoulders of management. Ultimately, the responsibility for all problems rises to the highest level of management.

Once you have completed your full investigation of the causes of your problems, the next thing is to review the true facts, and then determine the overall effects that these root causes have had on the problem at hand.

There will likely be some questions that can't be fully answered. However, once you believe that you have all of the pertinent facts together, you should start developing some of your alternative plans.

Planning & Implementing

Often, after making a full investigation you'll find that the real problem is not what you originally thought it was. You'll find out that what you first thought was the problem was actually only an indication or symptom of the real problem.

Always look for the real root causes of your problem. Treat the disease, not the symptom.

In most cases, there will be several courses of action you could take for solving any particular problem. However, there will be situations when you won't have the luxury of taking the time to check into each and every possibility. Take caution; don't make things worse by acting rashly.

Finally, selecting the best plan is the natural culmination of using all of the techniques that we've discussed thus far.

After you've narrowed down your possible alternatives, your final decision should then be influenced by what I have explained before as the **Worst-Case Factor**.

Determine, as best as you can, what is the worst thing that will happen if each of your plans of action were to fail completely. If you determine that you can live with the worst possible results, then you can safely risk any less than the most severe results from that plan. If not, immediately eliminate any alternative that doesn't pass this **Worst-Case** test.

After eliminating any alternatives that don't pass the **Worst-Case** test, then study the relationship of the expected results of each of the remaining acceptable plans to the overall risk of each plan; and pick the one that offers the best return for the least cost and least risk. Choose one plan and implement it.

Implementation marks the transition from the planning phase to the solution and review phase in the Success/Problem Cycle. Planning and problem solving is an ongoing process.

In my mind, planning and problem solving are like conjoined twins, somewhat different in their nature, but they share the same vital organs. The following tried and true sayings aptly describe the continuing nature of the problem solving cycle exceedingly well:

"If at first you don't succeed, try and try again."
"Nothing ventured, nothing gained."
"Back to the drawing board."

Very few things in life work out exactly as we plan. That's why problem solving is never over until you know that your plan has worked out completely to your satisfaction. If the results were not as productive as you expected, simply go back to the basics and start the process all over again.

There's nothing magical about people who do a good job of solving their problems. They're just persistent, and they have enough self-confidence and faith to fervently believe that somehow they will eventually get it right. Realistically, not even people with healthy self-images can solve every one of their problems without facing at least some undesirable consequences. The difference is that self-confident people usually handle whatever consequences they face, and they move on from there.

In the previous chapters we have primarily looked at the technical approach to planning and problem solving. Now we must focus our vision on the humanistic and philosophical side of decision-making.

Previously, I stated that the secret to effective management is predicated on understanding the five basic elements of having and acquiring useful knowledge, which I have taken the liberty of naming my concept the *Five Knows*. Specifically, I propose that all five of these aspects of knowledge and communication ability directly affect every person's decision-making ability.

As we have already established, gathering information is the key ingredient in all planning and problem solving. My concept of the *Five Knows* deals with the importance of self-confidence and intuition in the art of decision making.

The first positive mental state of mind that sets good decision makers apart is:

"Knowing what you know, when you know it."

In my experience, insecure people, with low self-esteem and little self-confidence, have a tendency to constantly second guess themselves. Many times they don't want to commit themselves to a particular point of view or general direction when looking for solutions to their problems. They may also tend to cover up their insecurity by not acknowledging their shortcomings. They dislike the process of gathering the information needed for any decision making job at hand. Invariably they procrastinate and vacillate.

On the other hand, I've found that people that are confident in understanding the limitations of their own knowledge don't seem to have a problem admitting that they need more information. They readily accept the second concept in the sequence:

"Knowing what you don't know,
when you don't know it."

Everyone knows what they don't know. People can't fool Mother Nature, and people can't really fool themselves either. Unfortunately, many people just can't bring themselves to be honest with themselves, and they try to get by with bluff and bluster. While I don't know who first said: "A little knowledge is a dangerous thing." I do know that they surely were right.

Trying to cover up the fact that you really don't know what you're doing will put you directly on the most traveled road to disaster. There's no shame is not knowing something you need to know. The shame is in making poor decisions by not finding out what you needed to know when the information was available.

When people have a high degree of faith in the knowledge that they truly have, they don't usually need to put up a false front. They value intellectual honesty, and they have no problem determining what they don't know.

Upon determining what you know, as well as what you don't know, logic leads us to the next phase of information gathering, which is probably the most critical step in all planning and problem solving:

"Knowing what you need to know."

This is the point at which most effective management practitioners engage in what some intellectuals call "Critical Thinking." It's the aspect of information gathering that requires us to seriously and systematically think in terms of exactly what we are trying to accomplish, and what resources we will need to accomplish our goals.

All people think differently and there is no magic model for critical thinking that meets all situations. In Street Smart terms, thinking critically involves using a systematic approach to gathering, weighing, and acting on, complete and accurate information.

This happens when you utilize the full power of my concept of *TMPT.* There is no substitute or alternative to giving extensive consideration to how *Time, Money, People, and Things* are related to your particular situation. Each one of these resources both affects and is affected by all of your decisions.

The better you are at delineating what you need to know, the better chance you will have at reaching the next level in the pursuit of knowledge:

"Knowing who knows
what you need to know."

For many of us "internet neophytes", this adage could be translated as: "Knowing who knows how to find the information on the Internet." In the fast paced electronic information age, I've been prompted by some to change this segment to read: "Knowing who or where to find out what you need to know." However, even the vast amount of information available on the Internet at the click of a mouse was, in truth, placed on the Internet by some real live person in the first place. And besides, I think the original wording sounds better.

Practically speaking, gathering all of the available technical facts under each segment of the TMPT model is only a portion of developing the total body of knowledge that you will need to know in order to make good

189

decisions. The major effort in gathering information will be in dealing with personal opinions. Facts alone mean nothing. In the end, it's your opinions about the facts that are critical. Reaching the point of sorting out opinions is when we reach the ultimate challenge in working with people:

"Knowing how to get them to let you know what they know."

The operative words to consider for getting others to tell you what you need to know are the building blocks of leadership: Trust, Loyalty, Influence, and Persuasion. We will discuss all of these important concepts in more detail in the upcoming chapters concerning empowerment and leadership.

At this point, I want to follow up the process of gathering information with a discussion of the philosophical aspects of making decisions. In addition to weighing all of the resources related facts and opinions, all decisions must also meet the intention of the company's mission statement, which should encompass full consideration of all of the attributes and entities covered by my notion of the "Loyalty Ladder."

THE LOYALTY LADDER

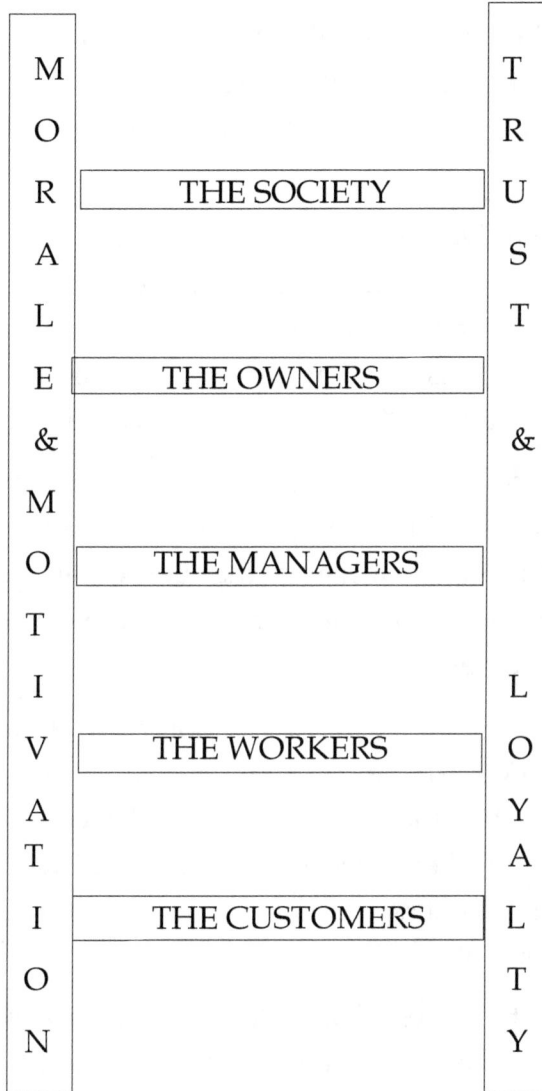

```
M                                    T
O                                    R
R    ┌──────────────────────────┐    U
A    │       THE SOCIETY        │    S
L    └──────────────────────────┘    T
E    ┌──────────────────────────┐
&    │       THE OWNERS         │    &
M    └──────────────────────────┘
O    ┌──────────────────────────┐
T    │      THE MANAGERS        │
I    └──────────────────────────┘
V    ┌──────────────────────────┐    L
A    │      THE WORKERS         │    O
T    └──────────────────────────┘    Y
I    ┌──────────────────────────┐    A
O    │     THE CUSTOMERS        │    L
N    └──────────────────────────┘    T
                                     Y
```

The "Loyalty Ladder" provides the basic framework for insuring that all decisions are in the best interest of the company and of everyone connected to the company.

The left side rail of the ladder is formed by the humanistic attributes of "Morale and Motivation." The right side rail of the ladder is formed by "Trust and Loyalty."

The fives rungs on the ladder are comprised by: The Society, The Owners, The Managers, The Workers, and the Customers and Suppliers. One way or another, every business decision that you will make will directly or indirectly affect every part of the *LOYALTY LADDER*.

Poor decisions, that adversely affect the workers' self-motivation, will frequently result in reducing the overall level of morale. Decisions that perpetuate poor morale will generally tend to stifle or reduce the workers' level of self-motivation even more.

Decisions that reflect poorly on the amount of trust the workers have in the company's management will surely lower the level of loyalty the company can expect from its workers. Decisions that indicate a lack of loyalty to the workers usually bring about a mistrust of management.

In the cases of *Morale and Motivation*, and *Trust and Loyalty*, there is usually a direct correlation between all four of these basic aspects of organizational behavior. If morale and motivation is down, so too will be trust and loyalty. As motivation goes up, so does morale. As trust and loyalty go up, morale and motivation usually follow.

In simple layman's terms, both side rails of the ladder are subject to change from any variation in either function within a side rail, and from any change in either factor in the other side rail.

Morale and Motivation and *Trust and Loyalty* can be thought of as the primary characteristics that define the humanistic spirit within any organization. If you have a tendency to think that troubles within these four intangible areas of organizational behavior are strictly internal problems, think again. The general public, customers in particular, are very quick to spot these types of problems within a company. Deficiencies in these areas rapidly manifest themselves in poor customer service.

The importance of weighing all management decisions, with respect to their effect on the *Society*, cannot be overlooked. Not only is it important to consider the legality of your decisions, you must also take into account such intangibles as: Ethics, morality, and principles.

A free society creates an open marketplace in which everyone has the opportunity to succeed. Business managers must insure that their decisions do not endanger the freedoms that we enjoy. Business must protect both the people and the environment from any lasting harm.

Good business managers understand that they must always be alert to avoiding decision which will result in the long range demise of their business. What do lumber companies do when they have cut down all the trees? They go out of business. How many cypress companies are still in existence in Louisiana? None!

The next rung on the ladder is dedicated to the welfare of the *Owners*. Why do we have to think about the effect of our decision on the owners? In a word, the answer is "money." Without adequate finances, no business can survive. Remember *TMPT!*

Most owners and investors are interested in a reasonable, long-term, return on their investment. This is where the idea of risk comes into play. Managers must carefully weigh the financial risk of every decision.

Many managers faced with poor profit performance look to drastic downsizing as a solution to what is in reality poor management performance. Wholesale efforts to cut the cost of labor at the risk of losing the entire business due to poor service and poor quality may not be such a good decision.

Sometimes managers have to do the hard thing. They have to spend more to make more. The answer to a poor bottom line performance may be to hire better people at higher wages, or to provide more training. A temporary reduction in cost, made for the wrong reasons, does not usually result in long-term prosperity.

The fact that the *Managers* rung is placed prominently in the middle of the ladder is no fluke. Managers provide the balance between the Society and Owners, on one side, and the Workers and Customers on

194

the other. Managers have the job of looking out for the interest of all, even themselves.

After all is said and done, managers must make decisions that are in the best interest of the company as a whole. Every decision made by every manager, at every level, of every organization, effects every rail and rung of the Loyalty Ladder. There's no other way to look at it.

In addition to making decisions that take into consideration all of the other entities represented on the ladder, managers must also make certain that they do not make decisions which either gives them too much authority or too little authority. And they must always take the full responsibility for every decision they make. Top management cannot escape having the ultimate responsibility for every decision made by every manager at every level below them.

The next rung down is dedicated to the *Workers*. Workers form the foundation of the organization. Without workers, nothing happens, goods and services don't get produced, and managers don't have anyone to manage.

Managers must be keenly aware of how their decisions will affect their workers. Within the ranks of the workers is where poor motivation, poor morale, lack of trust, and disloyalty most often result from poorly conceived decisions.

"Human Resources" is the supposedly enlightened term used to describe people in organizations today. Unfortunately, many managers still treat their people only like resources, not like humans. Your people will make you or break you. Treat them as people first, resources second.

Finally, no discussion of decision making would be complete without talking about the *Customers.* The equation is elemental:

NO CUSTOMERS = NO BUSINESS.

Knowing your customers and what they think is one of the most important areas of information you need for making decisions. I can't conceive of a situation where you would know too much about your customers.

Decisions that chase customers away usually come about from knowing too little about what your customers really want, and also what they are willing to pay for what they want. Customers aren't just interested in price; they also want dependability of quality, supply, and service. Many also want to know that the company they are buying from is a good member of the community.

Decisions that harm good customer relations will eventually hurt every other aspect of the company. When it comes to decisions and their affect on the customer, make this slogan your own:

CUSTOMER SATISFACTION

IS NUMBER ONE

Have we discussed everything there is to know about making decisions? No! And we never will. While there is important   value to using a systematic approach to gathering information, determining what the information means and its validity, developing alternatives, assessing risks, making decisions, implementing those decisions, and engaging in timely follow up, the truth is that decision making is an art that takes self-confidence, persistence, and a great deal of intuition.

I can guarantee that you will be prepared with the all of the basic ingredients for making good management decisions if you understand and follow these three major concepts I have presented to you:

1. **THE FIVE KNOWS**

2. **TMPT**

3. **THE LOYALTY LADDER**

I could have spent years filling up page after page in a book detailing hundreds of ways to look at the process of managing people and things. But, even if this book was a thousand pages thick, I couldn't change, or add to, the basic rules of the game. They have been the same since the beginning of time. They work now, and will remain the same for the rest of time.

As we proceed to the coming chapters, we'll delve into solving some of the different kinds of people and leadership problems you will often encounter in the real world of business.

CHAPTER 11

"In the Army"

No one succeeds in life all by themselves.

Empowerment is the hot word among management academics and philosophers. It's a pretty good word. People who use it sound like they went to college. The only problem is this: Many people confuse empowerment with the act of delegating authority. It's not the same. I look at empowering as a function:

A continuing process for giving people the opportunity to excel.

That might sound like an overly simplified definition, yet it defines what I consider the most fundamental and powerful force for effective people management.

I think the Army used to describe the empowerment process perfectly. (BE ALL THAT YOU CAN BE, IN THE ARMY). Their old slogan certainly expressed the human attraction to achieving personal excellence.

Whether or not the Army lived up to that slogan is open to wide debate. I'm sure many recruits would have something to say about it. However, lobbying for or against the Army is not my job.

Street Smart Managers understand that empowerment is monumentally important to the success of any joint venture.

Empowerment is unquestionably essential for team success; it should be encouraged even to the point of preparing your employees so well that they will eventually leave your company to achieve bigger and better things elsewhere. Good managers always encourage their subordinates to reach out and stretch towards reaching their greatest level of personal performance. Effective managers also constantly strive for excellence themselves.

In my experience, happy productive employees, normally leave a company only after they have grown well beyond their maximum potential for advancement within that company. Every company has some limitations on promotions and on the amount of salary it can offer its employees.

I have never begrudged a person for accepting a better opportunity elsewhere. Why should I? I've done it myself, and so would most other people I know. Wouldn't you?

In other words, people who out grow a company and move on to bigger and better things, only get better job offers because they have done a great job for their current employer.

The secret to effective empowerment is straight forward, hire the best people you can, let them excel, and keep them as long as you can. Steady growth comes from steady improvement.

As a company prospers and grows it should become more able to hire better employees, pay them more, and keep them longer.

Hiring people with low growth potential, simply because they'll remain in low-end jobs with limited opportunity for advancement, will certainly doom a company to an unstable and limited future.

Empowerment is an elusive process. It is not something you can touch. It's just like happiness. No one can empower you, and you can't force empowerment on anyone else. The principle ingredient of true empowerment is a two-way exchange of trust and loyalty.

Remember, as a manager the two-way process of empowerment is just as necessary for you as it is for your subordinates.

Real empowerment results from allowing people room to grow, not from forcing them to conform to harmful rigid limitations.

In itself, the act of delegating authority certainly doesn't encompass the full meaning of the whole process of empowerment. However, delegating authority and taking responsibility is an essential factor in effective empowerment.

Two policy areas affect the overall level of excellence that employees can achieve. The first area is the company's hiring philosophy, and the second is the company's overall policy for managing its employees. Each is equally important.

Webster's dictionary defines "mediocre" as: "of moderate or low quality."

Be careful not to equate the lasting effects of mediocrity with temporary inefficiency due to someone being untrained or lacking job knowledge.

Personal mediocrity is a condition that exists when a person, who may or may not have the innate ability to excel, has no interest in self-improvement.

It results from not having enough self-motivation to go beyond a low or moderate level of achievement. These kinds of people do not display productive behavior.

I have never found an acceptable answer to this question about a common hiring policy that certain companies follow: Why won't some companies hire a highly qualified person, and in many cases the most qualified person they could find, simply because that person has been in a more important or higher paying job in the past?

HR people generally label someone in this situation as being "Over Qualified."

I believe that the terminology "Over Qualified" is totally false. In reality, the term is often used to cover up a hiring bias of some kind. It probably used to mask age discrimination more often than any other type of bias.

Following this kind of policy can easily create a condition that I refer to as built-in mediocrity. Built-in mediocrity results when a company restricts its own ability to excel. It exists when people who have the ability to excel are kept from doing so, because of this type of counterproductive company policy and practice.

202

On the other hand, "Not Qualified", "Under Qualified", "Qualified", "Very Qualified", and "Highly Qualified" are all valid descriptive terms. "Over Qualified" doesn't even make sense.

I think claiming someone was "Over Qualified" really means that because of some biased reason, which they are probably unwilling to acknowledge, the person making the hiring decision was simply afraid to that hire that particular person.

It says more about the poor qualifications of the person doing the hiring than it does about the good qualifications of the person being considered for the job.

When mediocre managers hire mediocre employees, it perpetuates mediocrity. This cycle of incompetence also tends to produce restricted management vision.

A TIMELESS TIP

> **Companies only go as far
> as their employees take them.**

I can't think of one good reason why a company shouldn't hire a person that is the most qualified person they can find, regardless of their previous employment. I have always hired the most qualified person, even knowing that they would eventually move on.

Actually, I always hired the most qualified person who was willing to work for the money I could afford to pay. Many of those people had held higher paying and more prestigious jobs in the past, and I was glad to get them, when I could and for as long as I could.

Highly qualified workers do excellent work. Sure they move on, but at least you get more than your money's worth for the time they stay around. To me, that's a pretty good deal. It's a far better deal than getting less than your money's worth out of someone forever.

For many reasons, which I'll discuss later under the topic of teamwork, I advocate having the proposed immediate supervisor of any potential new employee have the final say in the hiring of that person.

Even in large companies, the human resource department should only check to see that the applicants meet the company's stated requirements for the job. The operating supervisors should make the final choice from the list of approved candidates.

The second management area that sustains built-in mediocrity falls under the training and development policies of the company.

A company should not only hire the best workers available, they should also do everything practical to allow their employees to become better than ever.

Lower and mid-level managers usually have the greatest influence in empowering new employees.

Why is it, that occasionally managers give someone a job and then do everything they can to make sure that the person fails in the job?

Time and time again, I've seen supervisors set their own workers up for failure. The sad thing is that most of the time they don't even realize that they're doing this.

The only explanation that makes any sense is that this type of manager is fearful that the very person whom they selected for the job will turn out to be the person who takes their job away from them.

Even self-employed persons need to make sure that they aren't placing any self-damaging restrictions on themselves.

As a manager, you must confront mediocrity in two directions:

o **Never place unwarranted restrictions on the people that work for you.**

o **Be careful to fight off non-productive restrictions placed on you.**

As each employee becomes more qualified, more trained, more enthusiastic, and more responsible for reaching their own peak performance level, the entire company becomes more effective and productive.

**Every person
in every position
in every company
is important
to the success of that company.**

I've always tried to associate with people who were smarter than I was. I've never stopped learning from them. I believe wanting to work for a boss who is not as capable as you are is a terrible mistake.

You may falsely think that working for an ineffective supervisor will make you look better by comparison. It doesn't work that way, and the long-range effects on your career will certainly be detrimental to you.

There are two splendid reasons why working for a highly competent and confident person is to your advantage: First, that person can teach you what you really need to know, and, secondly, self-confident people are seldom afraid to let others excel. In fact, they will generally be excited by and will be proud of your success.

Highly competent managers have very good, highly positive, healthy egos, and they operate from a position of rational self-confidence.

Conversely, mediocre bosses usually have poor self-images and they normally operate under the stress of an irrational fear of failure. Managers, who don't allow their workers to excel, never excel past a low level themselves.

At the beginning of this chapter we talked about delegating authority. Delegating authority is that portion of empowerment which allows people to take the responsibility for their actions. However, delegation of authority is not the beginning of the process of empowerment. Effective delegation is really the end product from the process of empowerment. Delegation is the fruit that the entire employee growing process bears.

206

Hiring the best employees available and placing them in employment conditions conducive to their development, while providing them with the opportunity to learn all that they can learn, evaluating their performance and their potential is crucial. Placing them in a job position that best fits their qualifications must all come before and lead up to the delegation of authority in the full sequence of empowerment.

Business risks are always present; yet, the best way to lose is to fail to prepare properly for the game. Never delegate authority to someone without having some idea of their ability to perform within the limitations of the authority which you plan to give them.

Street Smart Management isn't a dice toss. Before you delegate, check out the worst case scenario as we discussed in the chapter on problem solving. Setting specific parameters within which your subordinates can independently operate is an extremely crucial function of management.

Once you have delegated authority, it's essential to allow your subordinates to have the opportunity to make mistakes. There is a world of difference between inspiring your subordinates to strive for perfection and actually expecting perfection.

If you don't allow your subordinates to make a few less than perfect decisions occasionally, you'll end up making all of their decisions for them.

The only way to find out if people can really do something is to give them the chance to try it. Just be sure you're still around to pick up the pieces if things don't work out.

People who feel that they are not allowed to make mistakes will usually double-check with their superiors before making every decision.

Effective delegation involves knowing the capabilities of your subordinates and giving them authority that matches those capabilities. People need the authority to stretch their capabilities and keep on growing to their highest potential. However, it's overly risky to give someone authority that they are not prepared to handle.

It's far better to give a person broad decision making power within a rather limited area of responsibility, rather than giving them a broad range of responsibility with limited authority. Both authority and responsibility must be in balance. Untold problems result when a manager does not allow his or her subordinates to have full authority along with the full responsibility for their actions.

One person, or a small group of people, can only accomplish so much when they try to do everything by themselves.

Any company that does not create an effective empowerment system, along with the corresponding delegation of authority, will sooner or later exceed its limited level of competency. From then on, it's downhill!

A TIMELESS TIP

> **Good facilitators spend their time
> looking and listening, not doing.**

Street Smart Managers are facilitators. They provide oversight and support. I've spent most of my career trying to making the right decisions, about the right people, at the right time. Then I simply watched and waited for positive results.

So far, we've talked about providing leadership, maintaining a good positive self-image, communicating effectively, planning and setting goals, and solving problems.

True empowerment cannot take place without understanding that each of these activities is fundamental to the process of striving for excellence in management. When it comes to empowerment, I've saved my most important and perhaps most controversial thoughts till now. I call them my theory of:

Positive Turnover.

In short, not only should some employee turnover be expected, moreover, I've concluded that some turnover is a very positive result of effective empowerment.

209

In defense of my theory, I need to bring to mind the basics of business: Good business management is controlled by two fundamental requisites:

Making a sufficient profit,
and
staying in business forever.

If you don't make a sufficient profit, you won't be in business very long. If you're not in business very long, you won't make a sufficient return on the investment of your time and money. In short, you can never stop striving for excellence.

I propose that employee turnover is neither good nor bad in itself. It's the reasons for having low or high employee turnover that make the difference.

Employee turnover that is high and out of control is certainly not good. However, low turnover can be equally as bad when it is low only because there is no discipline and there are no quality standards in the company.

A great percentage of normal employee turnovers are directly related to the particular type of workers in the industry itself.

For example, retail stores and fast food restaurants normally have high turnover rates because they employ many temporary and part-time workers. This type of turnover is intrinsic to the type of work and the typical wage scale of the industry as a whole.

210

There's not much that a single manager can do to control the normal industry-wide turnover factor in their individual work environment. The only long-term solution to reducing the effects of this turnover problem is through empowerment.

Will empowerment eliminate employee turnover completely? No! In fact, as I've pointed out before, empowerment actually produces turnover in many cases.

If you're in an industry that has an expected high turnover rate, your real goal is to strive to maintain the lowest turnover rate among your local competitors.

The process for achieving this goal is to try to improve your ability to hire better qualified people than your competitors, and then trying to improve your ability to keep the best of those people from leaving, for as long as you can.

True empowerment includes everyone. Good managers not only empower their workers, they empower their customers, their suppliers, their owners, and their communities.

No one succeeds in life all by his or her self. Even people running a small business all by themselves must have some outside support.

There's no question that even a one-person business must have at least one customer and one supplier.

Street Smart Managers understand the full impact of these six concepts of empowerment:

Hire the highest qualified people.
Train your workers with your best people.
Let your workers accept responsibility.
Expect your workers to meet expectations.
Help workers solve their own problems.
Cheer your workers towards excellence.

In the next chapter, we'll explore the case for building positive working relationships that are guaranteed to create winners.

CHAPTER 12

"Cleared For Solo"

> People who fail in one situation
> seldom fail in all situations.

History is rife with stories about people who have reached great heights. Many of these famous people were lucky enough to have an early personal relationship with someone who played a very positive role in their lives.

Most people have their parents and other family members to help start them out on the road to success. Depressingly, in today's world the number of single parent families is increasing steadily, and many children are deprived of at least some of the security of a happy two-parent household.

This doesn't mean that orphans and children of dysfunctional households can't make it in the world of business. The world is full of people that have excelled in spite of abusive and horrific family situations. Besides, parents aren't perfect anyway.

Luckily, there are many opportunities in the working world to find mentors who can play important roles in your development. Some will play small parts and some will play leading roles in the shaping of your career.

I was very fortunate to have had two highly influential early mentors who were very closely involved in one of the most meaningful aspects of my adult life. Yet, they never even met each other.

Apart from my family, Charlie was my first real life-affecting mentor.

I met Charlie right after I had moved into the "Uptown" section of New Orleans. It was during the same time period in my life when I met Kenny, and Charlie lived in the house on the other side of Kenny's apartment.

Even though Charlie was nine years older than I was, Charlie was one of my best friends. As far as I was concerned, Charlie was the greatest.

Charlie was the oldest child in his family. He had two younger brothers and a younger sister, and they all lived at home with their mother and father.

Charlie built model airplanes. Not the motionless plastic models that just sit on a shelf, Charlie's planes really flew.

Over the years his skilled hands crafted large sail-planes, rubber-band powered planes, motor-powered models, U-controlled speedsters, and my all time favorites; the balsa wood hand-launched gliders that he designed himself.

We tend to think that money is the most valuable thing in life, but Charlie gave me something money couldn't buy. Charlie gave me his time, and he taught me so much more than just how to build model airplanes.

He taught me to enjoy learning new things, and how to meet new people.

He took me to air shows and to model airplane contests. Charlie literally took me under his wings.

Like most things in life, there were times when being Charlie's friend meant sharing the hard times too. I remember hearing a news report on the radio (we didn't have a TV in those days) about a tragic accident that happened over on the Audubon Park golf course.

A man playing golf had hooked a long drive off of the fairway into the rough. Without any warning, the errant ball struck a man who was leisurely walking through the park on a path next to the golf course. The ball struck his head and killed him instantly.

That unlucky golfer was Charlie's father. That poor man's death had a terrible affect on the whole family. It was a tragic freak accident, and it was something his father would never forget. The good memories far outweigh the bad.

I'll never forget that fantastic day in 1948, when Charlie took me to my first model airplane competition. Charlie helped me prepare for the contest, and he even paid my entrance fee. It was truly a day to remember.

There was a good breeze blowing when I faced into the wind and placed my fingers on the body of my handmade balsawood glider. It was one of Charlie's special designs. I held it just as he had taught me.

One, two, three steps and I launched my sleek little glider skyward, with all the might a skinny little twelve-year-old boy could muster.

Away it went, high up in the air. It swirled gracefully around the sky, descending ever so slowly, until it finally ran out of lift, and softly landed on the sweet smelling, freshly cut grass field.

Charlie's stop watch recorded the flight time at one minute and forty-nine seconds. The longest flying time in the hand-launched glider contest. I couldn't believe it was true. We had actually won.

Charlie really deserved all of the credit. The glider was built with his design. He helped me make it, and he taught me to send it skyward.

Charlie wasn't looking for any of the credit. When I went up to get the trophy, Charlie was thrilled. I believe he was more proud of me than I was. Charlie was a great mentor. Mostly, I remember the good times with Charlie.

He taught me pride of craftsmanship. He taught me dedication and the true value of joy and enthusiasm. He taught me that winning was fun, but that it wasn't the most important thing in life. The fun was in the trying. When you help someone else to become a winner, you feel just as proud and excited as they do.

That hand-launched glider trophy is nearly a half-a-century old now, and a little beat up from a lifetime of travel. I think about Charlie every time I see it, and when I look back, I find that lots of people have influenced my life. Most of them for the good and some not so good, but I've learned from those experiences too.

After nearly fifty years, while I was writing this book, I finally realized that the main reason I became an Air Force pilot was because of Charlie's influence in my life.

Charlie's influence was always good. Charlie was one of my earliest mentors. He taught me much more than I realized at the time. He taught me three timeless lessons:

It's more fun to give than to receive.
It's far greater to love than to be loved.
Life goes on no matter what,
so take it one day at a time.

Charlie planted the seed of flight, and just about eleven years later, in a different time and a different place, a real true guardian angel came along to raise me up on silver wings.

My angel's name was Captain Kent Cooley. He literally flew in to my life just when I really needed him the most. Charlie first taught me how to fly model airplanes, and then Captain Cooley taught me how to soar above the clouds in the real ones.

The whole story is that the good Captain didn't just teach me how to fly; he saved me from washing out of flight school.

I'll gladly tell anyone that earning my wings as a pilot in the United States Air Force was, and still is, the hardest thing I've ever done. Most of the other student pilots in my class had a ball in flight school, but not me. For me, it was all business, and a life threatening business at that.

I married in my last year of college, and by the time I entered flight school, my first baby was on the way. Having another mouth to feed meant that getting my wings wasn't just for fun, it was an economic necessity.

I had to make it through flight training, or lose my flight pay and spend the next four years stuck in the Air Force at one fourth less salary. That was not a pleasant thought. Not only was I worried about washing out, I also gave more than one passing thought to the extremely unpleasant possibility of a fatal crash, or maybe if I was lucky, just having to bail out.

From the moment my instructor first declared that I was "Cleared for solo", I knew I was taking my life in my hands every time I left the ground. My life and my career were on the line, and the pressure for achieving a high degree of excellence was overwhelming and unrelenting.

Most of my flying grades very fairly high, but at one point near the end of my training program I was having lots of problems trying to master the art of formation flying. It took a great toll on my nerves.

I visited the base infirmary so many times that the nurses had memorized my name, rank, and serial number. I survived by drinking a mixture of Kaopectate and Paregoric almost every day for the entire year. The flight surgeons called it "liquid cork."

Lt. Cutrer, my initial formation flight instructor, was a top-notch pilot and truly a good guy. He could fly the old "T-Bird" jet fighter trainer with the best of them. Fred was a good old boy from Mississippi, and I was from the bayou country of Louisiana.

Personally we got along great. Fred liked me and I liked him. He tried his best to teach me how to fly in tight formation. Unfortunately, the more he tried the worse I flew. And the worse I flew, the louder he got.

Somehow, it seemed like he got louder in geometric proportions. Whenever I did something wrong, his normal teaching method was to add more volume and greater profanity to his instructions. It was definitely instruction by intimidation.

My response to his ranting and raving was greater and greater fright, and worse and worse tense flight. Unfortunately, as teacher and student, we just didn't hit it off. He could fly so proficiently that he just couldn't understand why I was doing so badly.

Patience wasn't his greatest virtue. I was so tense when I was flying with him that you couldn't pry my hand off of the control stick with a crowbar.

Sweat poured off my face. My control motions were so jerky that the plane was never in the right position at the right time. Not even for a nano-second.

I was a nervous wreck. I not only feared failure, I constantly feared for my very life. I clearly knew that there was no such a thing as a slight collision between two jet planes going through the air at hundreds of miles per hour. That terrifying thought was always there, stuck firmly in the back of my mind,

My nerves were so frayed that I couldn't fly a kite much less a high-speed jet plane just a few feet away from another one.

Fred finally figured I would never make it through formation flight training, and he reluctantly put me up for a washout check ride.

That was it. It was my last chance. I had finished all of the other flight training segments with pretty good grades, but if I couldn't pass the formation phase, nothing else counted. Flight school would be history.

My self-image was pretty badly out of focus, and I definitely wasn't having very much fun. That's when my faithful guardian angel took me under his wing.

Captain Cooley was a "Standboard" pilot, one of the dreaded check ride pilots who held every student's future in their hands. They gave no quarter, and to make sure they were sufficiently intimidating they wore solid black flight suits. Behind their backs, we called them the Greenville Gestapo.

Facing a final graduation check ride was awesome in itself, but facing an early wash-out check ride was frightening beyond belief. I was petrified, and I showed it.

I don't know how I made it through that check ride. I'm sure it was only by the mercy of God and Captain Cooley's pity.

I can't really say that I remember exactly what happened during that flight. It's still all a blur in my brain. Luckily, the Captain evidently saw something in me that told him I could make it, and instead of washing me out, he volunteered to take over as my instructor.

Captain Cooley's name fit him perfectly. As both a pilot and as a person he was the epitome of calm, cool, and collected. He had been a top fighter pilot in Korea, and nothing this side of war bothered him. He was the most confident and competent pilot I've ever known.

He straightened me out during the first lesson. By the end of the flight, I was flying close formation like never before. When the lead plane's jet wash made my plane's rudder shake in its exhaust, I knew I was finally flying in tight trail formation.

Flying with my angel during those following weeks was the most fun I've ever had in an airplane. My self-confidence was fully restored, and I felt that I could soar like an eagle.

He showed me how to fly with confidence, with a light touch, making slow, smooth, and deliberate stick movements, with only the tip of my thumb and index finger touching the control stick. Once I mastered that technique, I could have flown close formation with a flock of wild geese going south for the winter.

Captain Cooley did such a good job of teaching me that he couldn't shake me off of his tail during twenty minutes of a wild, twisting, turning, all out aerial dog-fight during my final formation check ride.

By the time I graduated and got my wings, I had gone from almost packing my bags, to finishing flight school with one of the highest flying grades in the class. Captain Cooley taught me that persistence is 99% of what it takes to win.

221

A TIMELESS TIP

> **Winners encourage.**
> **Losers discourage.**

Just like Charlie had done when I was a child, Captain Cooley also taught me some of his valuable secrets. He wasn't afraid to give away some of what he had. He empowered me to become the best pilot that I could be.

Like I've said before, I'm a very lucky man.

Early in my military career, I learned that the best leader you can have is the smartest, most capable, most understanding, and most secure leader you can find. I've never forgotten that lesson.

When I became an instructor pilot myself, I always remembered what Captain Cooley had done for me, and I eventually had the chance to help someone else in a similar situation.

"What goes around comes around." That's another great old saying too, isn't it?

My job at Mather Air Force Base was to check out new pilots in the twin engine "T-29" Convair, and because I always remembered the affect Lt. Cutrer had on me, I tried to make sure that I wasn't a voice raiser when I had a new student in the airplane.

I'll have to admit, I finally blew my stack when I just couldn't get this one new pilot to understand that flying directly across the path of another airplane wasn't such a wise idea. He was spending too much time with his eyes in the cockpit, eye-balling his instruments, and not enough time looking out of the window for other aircraft and the runway. That can be a deadly mistake.

One day, we had a very close near miss when he made a turn directly in front of a monstrous four engine "C-124" on its final approach to the field. The "C-124" was the biggest cargo plane the Air Force had at the time.

I reacted instantly. I took control of the plane and narrowly avoided a mid-air collision. After getting out of the flying monster's way, I landed the plane immediately. We taxied to the parking ramp without a word being said between us. I think it was the longest ten minute taxi ride he ever had.

I won't repeat all of the comments I made to him that day, but I did tell him in no uncertain terms: "If you want to kill yourself, that's up to you; but I'm damn sure not going to let you kill me."

I finally got his attention by refusing to fly with him again. I knew that he could fly; he just needed to be more concerned about safety and less concerned about perfection.

He was a good officer, and I knew we really needed him in our squadron. That's why I asked my good friend and fellow instructor, Don Grigsby, to take over as his instructor.

Once again, a change of instructors did the trick, and he eventually became one of our best pilots. Actually, I did fly with him many times afterwards, and I was very proud to do so. I was glad that I knew what it meant to be given a second chance.

Many people make the mistake of giving up on a person without giving someone else a chance to work with them. Compatibility is one of the most crucial aspects of successful teamwork and supervision.

The negative effects of incompatibility are extremely powerful. That's the reason why I so strongly advocate hiring policies that allow all immediate supervisors to make the final selection of all employees who will work under them.

A true mentor/mentee relationship exists between supervisors and the people who work for them.

Not only must supervisors set the example, they must also fulfill the role of mentor when they evaluate their employee's performance.

Many managers don't realize the impact of the employee evaluation process. Employees can only reach their ultimate potential when they fully understand the company's expectations.

I learned two very valuable business lessons from my Air Force flying days.

Lesson One: Not all people relate to each other in productive ways.

Lesson Two: People who fail in one situation, seldom fail in all situations.

Both unnecessary resource dissipation and inhibited growth potential results from failing to understand how these two lessons relate to business management in the real world.

A personnel evaluation system that only identifies deficiencies and only indicates whether or not a person has met some minimum standard of acceptability does not fulfill the true role as a tool for employee empowerment. Furthermore, even the company's training and evaluation system itself must continuously be evaluated and improved upon. Street Smart Managers continually evaluate themselves as well as their workers.

Meaningful and honest evaluations produce positive results, while poor, incomplete, and biased evaluations stifle productivity and growth. The more care you give to the evaluation function of management, the more successful you will be.

As a manager, you will have to deal with the evaluation function in two ways: 1) Evaluating your subordinates, and 2) Acting on the evaluations made of you by your superiors.

225

Grading the job knowledge phase of an employee's evaluation can be accomplished by quantitative and mechanical means. Written test on the subject matter and demonstrations of the employee's physical capabilities for performing the physical work are two such methods. However, job knowledge and performance potential alone are not the only indicators of an employee's full worth.

Just because someone possesses the ability to perform a certain job well doesn't mean that having the ability alone will have a great affect on determining whether or not that person will actually do an excellent job, or even be a good employee.

On the other hand, a person who exhibits the basic capacity to perform a job well, and who also displays dedication, cooperation, loyalty, drive, and a full commitment to excellence; will generally outdistance a person who has greater natural ability, but lacks sufficient motivation and responsibility. Street Smart Managers evaluate potential as well as performance.

No matter what type of personnel evaluation system your company uses, it will always be subject to the biases of the persons doing the evaluating.

Mediocre managers generally produce mediocre evaluations. They may not even be able to recognize potential any higher than their own limited experience provides.

Excellent managers, with good positive self-images, can not only give valid and meaningful evaluations to deserving workers, they can also give excellent guidance to employees who want to improve their performance.

Evaluations must always be as fair and as impartial as possible. However, regardless of the evaluation system used in your company, there are many elements of a person's performance and behavior that are highly subject to variations in the personal opinions of the evaluators. After considering all of the different human flaws inherent in any kind of an evaluation system, I still believe that even the worst evaluation system is better than none.

There are many variations and subsets of job related factors that can be evaluated. In essence, they can all be reduced into the following four principal areas:

Mental and Physical Capacity
Work Habits and Efforts
Performance Stability
Work-Group Relationships

Whenever a deficiency is reported in any of these four major areas, the evaluator should always give the person a reason for the deficiency, and make suggestions for eliminating or reducing it.

I'll conclude by saying that an evaluation system should be used as a tool for empowerment, not as a tool for holding down raises and perpetuating the status quo.

Yes Virginia, this book does come to an end with Chapter 13, and I've saved the best stuff for the last chapter.

Since I was born on the 13th, I've never thought of it as an unlucky number. Maybe that's why I take more risk than I should.

The topic for the last chapter is "Teamwork." Teamwork puts it all together. Everything we've talked about in this book comes in to play in the process of creating successful teams and teamwork is what gets the job done.

When all is said and done, like we say in the Big Easy:

Teamwork
is where it's at!

CHAPTER 13

"Go Team Go"

> **Good for you!   Good for me!
> Good for us!**

Planning Teams, Work Teams! Performance Teams! Executive Teams! Team Leaders! Team Facilitators! Everybody's talking about teams. It's as if teamwork has just been discovered, and the whole world is jumping on the teamwork band wagon. Teams are really hot stuff!

In truth, there's really nothing at all new about teams. Teams aren't even a phenomenon of the industrial revolution. Teams are as old as mankind, and history shows that civilization itself is the natural development of the fruits of teamwork.

Give people a common problem, and they'll try to solve it together. Furthermore, people seem to work together better under adversity than they do in times of prosperity.

Teams function at their best when the team leaders truly understand the great power generated from the combined energy or force resulting from a superior personal performance by every member of the team.

Today's survival-of-the-fittest worldwide economic marketplace demands pragmatic managers.

The New Lexicon Webster's Dictionary of the English Language describes teamwork this way:

Teamwork, n. the quality whereby individuals unselfishly subordinate their own part to the general effort of the group with whom they are working or playing.

If you accept this staid definition as fact, you probably believe that teamwork requires each and every individual to hold back or reduce their own performance, because it's not nice to exceed the abilities of any of the other team members

You might even believe that, just for the sake of maintaining harmony, all coaches, from the little leagues to the pros; should hang this warning sign over their locker room doors:

NOTICE
SUPERSTARS NEED NOT APPLY

Don't believe that for a minute. Smart coaches want every superstar they can get, and professional teams pay big bucks to get them.

I contend that a philosophy that calls for restricting individual performance, in any way, is totally counterproductive to group efficiency and effectiveness.

I think it's one hundred and eighty degrees out of phase with what real teamwork is all about. That kind of backward thinking is only guaranteed to do one thing:

Create losers!

Winning teams win because the team leaders appreciate and acknowledge the value of each and every person on the team, regardless of the differences in their talent and productivity. Smooth running teams are fueled by the total amount of accumulated energy coming from each person's individual best performance.

Each and every member of the team must be allowed to function at a high and consistent level of performance.

When one or more members of the team are not routinely performing up to their normally expected capacity, the team's engine losses power and can't pull the load.

Technically speaking, a team is simply two or more people banded together in a common pursuit. Anybody can be on a team.

Some managers think that they can develop teamwork by simply assigning people to a team, and ordering them to complete a job by working together. Too bad it isn't that easy. Let me quickly offer this caution: There is a huge difference between assigning people to a team and developing successful teamwork.

Well trained team members support each other. They strive for personal excellence, while at the same time helping their team mates in the process.

Winners understand that the best way to get support is to give support. They play by the same old dependable "Golden Rules."

Lasting leadership is based on mastering this timeless and simple prescription for success. Furthermore, it's a waste of time to talk about building teams until you master the basics of successful personal relationships.

Teamwork is a dynamic process, which must be cultivated and nurtured. It takes individual initiative and continuing support.

Effective leadership and efficient teamwork doesn't just happen. On the other hand, successful teamwork results automatically when you understand and practice all of the Street Smart Management principles that we've covered in the first twelve chapters.

In the real world, the ultimate sign of a team's success is found when a team has actually effectively and efficiently accomplished a meaningful task.

In my experience, winners usually win in no small part, because they are having fun. Winners certainly don't like it when they occasionally lose, but win or lose; they have fun playing the game.

Achieving real teamwork takes deliberate, logical, and enthusiastic preparation.

Experience shows that teamwork reaches its peak performance when the team is well coached and well prepared.

This takes self-confidence, good leadership, effective communication, and proper planning.

Since I have branded Webster's definition of teamwork as misleading, I'll offer my own:

Teamwork, n. the quality whereby individuals join together to achieve a worthwhile common goal, and devote their best individual effort to achieving that goal, both efficiently and effectively.

My definition stresses using the best individual effort of each team member, in order to complete a task in both an efficient and effective manner. The principle of all teamwork dictates putting together a group of people who have all of the necessary talent, ability, and self-motivation to perform the task at hand.

Even when a team leader attempts to avoid all of the obvious pitfalls that prevent success, there is no guarantee that a team leader's effort to cultivate a successful team will bear fruit.

Nobody can guarantee successful team leadership, but it is relatively easy to present a litany of reasons why many teams frequently fail.

All of us have seen teams of people seemingly doing all of the right things; still they fail to achieve their goals. Yet, many times, other teams seem to achieve success by doing things that appear on the surface to be exactly the same kinds of things as the teams that fail.

So, just how do you start to build a team that really works? The clues are found in these four fundamental truisms that influence all teamwork:

The principles of teamwork are elementary.
Yet, effective team leadership is complex.
All people are similar.
Yet, all people are different.

Each of these four statements might, at first glance, appear somewhat contradictory to each other, but in reality, each independent statement is undeniably true. Taken together, these rock solid statements describe the essence of all teamwork and human relations.

After considering why many teams don't win, I've come up with the following list of fundamental reasons why winning teams don't materialize:

Teamwork doesn't happen when there is no leadership.

Teamwork doesn't happen when members of the team lack self-confidence.

Teamwork doesn't happen when there is poor communication among the team members.

Teamwork doesn't happen when there is poor planning and faulty goal setting.

Teamwork doesn't happen when the team doesn't recognize and solve their problems.

Teamwork doesn't happen until every individual on the team is empowered and encouraged to strive for personal success.

The following basic principles of teamwork show us why developing and maintaining highly productive teams is more of a social art than a scientific undertaking. Let's take a look at each of these four clauses.

The principles of teamwork are elementary.

The underlying principle of teamwork is essentially this: In order to accomplish a task in the least costly and least time consuming manner, group tasks can usually be performed more efficiently, less costly, and in the shortest period of time, by getting a number of capable people working together, as efficiently as possible.

Group success is more easily accomplished, by using each person's talents and abilities to the group's best advantage.

The team leader assumes the responsibility for creating conditions that allow the whole team to perform in the most effective, least costly, and least time consuming manner.

Yet, effective team leadership is complex.

If the principle behind teamwork is so elementary, why then is team leadership so complex? Because, life itself is complex.

Nothing stays the same. Everything changes constantly. The weather changes. Society changes. People change. Change is the main force that makes team leadership complex.

Change means that you have to learn to roll with the punches, hang in there, pick up the pieces; and keep on playing the game. You can't win if you throw in the towel.

Effective leadership involves constant observation, planning, and adjusting. Don't expect perfection. You'll go crazy looking for something that doesn't exist. Just keep on trying till something works, then try to make it work better. There is no status quo, and nothing is perfect.

There's nothing more complex than a human being, and all teams are made up of human beings. Fortunately, every leader has the same complexities of life to deal with. Your competitors in business have the same human circumstances to deal with as you have.

All people are similar.

Earlier, I made the case that all people need to survive, feel safe, be secure, feel like they belong, and have self-esteem. And in the end, all people need to feel that they have actually accomplished something with their lives.

These similarities provide the answer to why teams got started in the first place. It's apparent that each of our basic needs can usually be met more easily through a communal or team effort. It was surely easier to gather food and build shelters when there was help.

236

The beneficial affect of having one or more helpers is easy to recognize when we look at a person's need to accomplish something. People can generally accomplish more, in less time, when they have help.

Our social and biological needs stem from our natural biological urge to reproduce. Since it "Takes Two to Tango", I think we can safely surmise that the earliest teams were made up of at least two people.

Self-esteem is important, because it gives people a feeling of equality among others. Within a group situation, a secure sense of equality is necessary for people to function satisfactorily.

Teamwork was born out of people's basic similarities. It's the natural and continuing evolution of humanity's drive to meet their basic needs. "You help me and I'll help you."

Yet, all people are different.

Even though all people have the same universal needs, their similarities end when it comes to each individual's own means, manner, and self-motivation for meeting those needs. Certainly no two people are the same when it comes to each one's biological, sociological, and psychological make-up.

Thank God for diversity. Street Smart Managers place emphasis on celebrating people's differences, not on attempting to make everyone conform to a common mold of mediocrity.

Diversity is the key element in developing highly efficient and productive teams.

Diversity allows us to balance the strengths and weakness of the various individuals on the team. People bring diverse amounts of ability, drive, and productivity to the team. You'll be ahead of the game if you don't even expect everyone to contribute equally. It doesn't happen.

On the other hand, no matter how large or small a contribution one person makes, every team member is important to the overall success of the team.

Winning coaches know that each member of a team brings with them varying degrees of talent, training, and temperament. They know that the real force behind a winning team comes from harnessing the energy of all of the people involved, including the bench warmers.

In the working world, every leader must understand that each person, in their own special way, is important to the success of a company.

Smart leaders use every resource they have. Many times, workers will contribute much more than they are initially given credit for. Some people have a way of fooling you when you write them off too quickly. The story of my friend, Henry, very clearly illustrates this point.

Henry was in his early forties. He was a working dynamo, about five feet ten inches tall, with arms of steel and a body that could qualify him for a shot at the title of Mr. Universe.

There wasn't an ounce of fat on his body. He was as strong as an ox, and he could outwork anybody in the plant. Plant workers were occasionally given colorful nicknames by their fellow workers.

Floyd, one of Henry's fellow workers, because at one time he was the newest man in the plant, even though he had been working there for about eight years when I arrived on the scene, was still called "Green Man."

My moniker was "Boss Man." There's no telling what they called me when I wasn't in the room. When it came to having descriptive nicknames, Henry was no exception. Everybody called him "Wild Man." Even his wife called him Wild Man. I never heard anybody call him Henry in the six years I worked there.

Admittedly, when I first heard the name "Wild Man", it didn't exactly conjure up visions of someone who would be a congenial, cooperative, and committed member of a smooth running company team.

I was told that he had gotten the name when he first started working at the refinery, and that it very accurately described his most memorable behavior pattern.

Wild Man was hired on as a plant laborer. It was the lowest job classification in the union contract. Like Robert, he couldn't read or write either.

As the story goes, when some of the other workers first found out that Henry was illiterate, they decided they would take advantage of him. On his first payday, they told him his paycheck was for a lesser amount than it really was, and they offered to cash it for him for twenty dollars less than the correct amount.

He agreed to the offer, and took the cash. The workers who played the prank thought it was a big joke. His wife didn't. I was told that this check cashing rouse only happened once.

From then on, his wife came to the refinery to pick up his paycheck every Friday. Some of the workers thought they could prolong the fun, by teasing him about his wife coming to pick up his check.

Then they made the incredibly foolish mistake of teasing him in front of his wife. Naturally, he couldn't let that kind of mean spirited challenge to his manhood go unanswered.

The story tellers told me he literally went wild with anger. He screamed and hollered, jumped up and down, ranted and raved, and chased his foolish tormentors throughout the refinery with an ax.

Over the next few paydays it continued to be great sport for the other workers to see if they could once again cause his outrageously wild behavior. I'm told that, for a while, it happened each time he got paid.

The teasing eventually stopped, but the name stuck, and his story became a vital part of the refinery's folklore.

After relating the story of how he got his name, it might sound a little off-the-wall when I say that the Wild Man I knew was always a gentleman. Actually, nobody ever really dared to challenge Wild's manhood. They knew better.

In his own way, I believe that Wild was just playing along with the group, in order to be accepted. He never really caused any trouble, and he never hurt anyone.

In reality, Wild was a good, dependable, and steady worker. He was a real company man, and I sincerely liked him. He had a positive self-image, and he loved serving others.

The real point to my story isn't about how he got his name. The real moral to the story is that this same man, who couldn't read or write, ended up saving the company thousands and thousands of dollars.

Wild was a maintenance man. His job was to keep eight huge asphalt oxidizing kettles operating efficiently.

Each of the kettles was about forty feet long and ten feet in diameter. They were large round tanks, mounted on their sides. Both ends had a twenty-four inch round hatch, which could be opened for access to the inside.

On the inside of each kettle were two sets of four inch round air-tubes, that ran lengthwise along the bottom of the tank.

The air-tubes were mounted about eighteen inches above the bottom of the kettles, and they ran in both directions from a central compressed air supply pipe. There was also a twelve inch round fire-tube on each end of the tank.

Natural gas burners were placed in these fire tubes and were used to heat the asphalt to a molten state, at nearly five hundred degrees Fahrenheit.

Compressed air blew through the air tubes near the bottom of the tank, and the air then percolated up through the asphalt. This created an oxidizing process, which changed the physical properties of the asphalt.

Using this process, the company produced a multitude of products, including: roofing asphalt, paving asphalt, waterproofing agents, and many asphalt coatings and adhesives. The company promoted itself as the "World's Largest Specialty Asphalt Manufacturer."

The constant high heat in the tanks produced a rock solid substance we called "coke" that would build up all around the inside of the tanks. The coke was an unwanted by-product. It would cling to the bottom of the tanks, and eventually clog up the air tubes. At that point the tanks could no longer be used.

Wild's main job was periodically removing about two feet of solid coke, which would build up under and in between all of the tubes inside of tanks.

Wild and one helper would get inside of a tank with pick axes, shovels, and buckets. The other helper would stay outside to carry off the buckets of coke as they were being chipped away, and handed to him from the inside, bucket by bucket.

It was the hardest and hottest job in the plant. It took three workers almost a month to clean out just one tank. This same labor intensive and time consuming method had been used by the company for over twenty-five years.

Shortly after I was put in charge of the refinery operations, I went out into the plant to see how the kettle cleaning operation worked. Wild Man enthusiastically responded to all of my questions about his job. He was just waiting to talk to someone that would listen to him.

He made a very practical suggestion that he believed would greatly reduce our maintenance cost and dramatically improve our production capability.

He was excited. He promised me that if we would just try his idea, he could reduce the cleaning time from a full month, to no more than one week in each tank.

Wild's suggestion was pretty simple. He wanted to use an air compressor and a ninety-pound jackhammer to loosen the coke from under the air tubes. He was convinced that he could remove the coke at a faster rate than doing it by hand. His idea worked great.

I estimated that Wild's idea saved the company at least thirty thousand dollars a year in maintenance costs, and improved our production capacity by at least fifty percent.

The idea was so obviously workable, why hadn't anybody tried it before? Nobody ever bothered to ask for Wild's opinion. After all, how could a man who couldn't read or write have any ideas that were worthwhile?

A TIMELESS TIP

> **Hidden potential often outweighs
> visible disability.**

Nobody had stopped to realize that Wild Man possessed the hard earned wisdom of practical experience. He was the one faced with the dirty job, each and every day. Wild taught me a valuable lesson about the difference between book learning and natural intelligence.

Here's another wise old saying that always makes sense:

It takes all kinds of people to make a world.

The moral of the story is simple: People count even when they can't.

Never (dis)count anyone too quickly.

With the pros and cons of diversity in mind, just how do you develop teamwork? Experience leads me to believe that the key word for building and maintaining an effective team is:

COMPATIBILITY

Except for the basic requirement that all team members must at least have the minimum required job knowledge, and the ability to perform the task at hand, nothing else matters more than compatibility.

Compatibility reduces mutual contradiction, and offsets any potential unbalancing of the energy taking place among the team members. In plain words, compatibility keeps everyone pushing in the same direction, at the same time.

Compatibility between a person's own mind and body is what I call:

Internal Compatibility

This internal compatibility requires continuity between the internal thoughts and the external actions of each individual member on the team, especially the leader. It means that a person's mind and body must work in unison.

Building a successful team starts with a team leader who has a strong, positive, self-image. Leaders can't have internal conflicts, which can create real-life contradictions between their thoughts and actions. A positive self-image is mandatory for anyone in a leadership role, at every level of management.

When it comes to maintaining fully productive relationships between a leader and his or her team, internal integrity is much more important than outward appearances. Phonies don't last long.

Leaders who actually practice what they preach have many common traits. They have a high degree of self-confidence and strong self-motivation. They appreciate loyalty, and they trust others. They also truly enjoy their work. If you want others to believe in you, you must believe in yourself.

Members of the National Speakers Association, who make their living by telling others how to live happy and successful lives, all vow to try to live by this often quoted NSA motto:

"Walk the walk, and talk the talk."

True balance between what a leader says and what a leader really believes is the only thing that gives long lasting value to their leadership.

Self-confidence allows a leader to freely encourage others to perform at their best. Self-confident leaders don't fear competition from their own team members, and they get added enjoyment from watching their team members reap the joy and rewards of their productivity.

On the contrary, if someone doesn't think they can be effective in their team role, then the probability that they will be very effective is close to zero. Self-esteem is the key to being able to portray the self-confidence that is needed to inspire others.

Let's look at some of the reasons why leaders have problems, and how these problems are directly related to low levels of self-esteem:

- **Leaders, who don't think they can win, surely won't.**
- **Leaders that don't appreciate and display trust and loyalty can't expect to receive trust and loyalty.**
- **Leaders that have little self-motivation will impede motivation in others.**
- **Leaders, who find no joy in their work, kill the joy for everyone.**

If deep down inside, someone on the team doesn't care if they succeed, that person surely won't make a positive contribution to the team. Worse yet, if a person subconsciously wants to fail, he or she will definitely cause all kinds of negative dynamics within the team.

In additional to "Internal Compatibility", teamwork also requires compatibility with, and among, all of the members of the team. I call this phenomenon:

External Compatibility

External compatibility describes a positive state of congeniality. Congeniality creates harmony, which allows the various team members to work together in a manner which promotes true success for all. Simply put, everyone on the team must be able to get along with each other.

Peace and harmony on a team comes from true compatibility. It doesn't come from making everybody on the team conform to the exact same standards.

Restricting the performance of individuals on the team creates resentment, not congeniality.

Total resource involvement comes about only when all members of the team are considered equally important to the group activity. Compatibility is so crucial to success that we must always be aware of its two-edged opposite force. This Jekyll and Hyde element of teamwork is commonly known as:

Competition

With very few exceptions, engaging in competition with other businesses is necessary for economic survival.

Team facilitators, supervisors, managers, department heads, directors; or whatever your company calls them, are the front-line officers in the war of economic competition.

Successful team leaders constantly train and prepare their troops for the real battle: Economic Competition.

Meeting competition from an outside force is constructive and productive. In all forms of economic warfare, just as in nature, only the fittest will survive.

Conversely, encouraging competitiveness within your own team can be destructive, and even potentially disastrous in some cases. I say don't do it! It's sort of like eating wild mushrooms. There's so little value to it, it's not worth taking the chance that your team will die of poisoning from within.

The problem with competition between members of the same team is that it frequently becomes an effort to win at all cost for one person or one team. Winning at all cost usually means that the winner wins, but only at the expense of everybody else on the team, and many times the whole team loses.

Competition, that pits one team member's ego against any others, can easily destroy congeniality. Remember, congeniality removes conflict and stress from interpersonal relationships.

When everyone truly strives for team success, it cultivates collegiality, and enhances congeniality. Congeniality is the trademark of happy people. When it comes to success, happiness is it.

Regarding the relationship between the leader and the other members of the team, just who has to be compatible with whom? There's only one practical answer: All team members have to be compatible with the team leader.

A good leader is usually able to cope with many types of personalities. However, if someone on the team proves to have a personality that just doesn't fit in with the team leader's job related personality, then for the sake of the team and everybody on it, that person has to go.

This sounds like a dictatorial theory of management doesn't it? In a way it is. In practice, when the overall welfare of the team is at stake, a good team leader must be a benevolent dictator.

I believe that all people do everything they do for selfish reasons, and rightly so. The reason people give lots of time and money to charity is because it makes them feel good. Sometimes it feeds their ego, other times it eases their guilt. Generally, it's either one or the other.

My theory of positive selfishness might sound somewhat anti-social, but, in my way of thinking, selfishness, in the honest pursuit of team success, is a very good thing, as long as the leader controls it.

As I said before: **"A house divided cannot stand."** Good leaders understand how this concept fits into the reality of life. When a team fails, it doesn't do anyone any good. Everyone loses!

In plain language, everyone on a team has to be along for the ride, work along to reach the destination; and get along, along the way.   There's no doubt about it, compatibility goes a long, long, way.

In the fierce battle of economic competition, teamwork is all about winning. Productive teamwork makes everybody a winner, and everybody wants to be a winner.

All people who work for the same company benefit from that company's prosperity.

A TIMELESS TIP

> **People who enjoy working together usually work together very well.**

Working to achieve a worthy common goal is good for everybody. Cheerleaders for all teams should jump up and shout this rousing cheer:

Good for you!
Good for me!
Good for us!

Some people think that teamwork is a process that is confined to individual departments within a company. They take the attitude that it's their department against the rest of the company. This commonly occurs within many companies, and often results in severe problems.

A company isn't made up of just one individual work crew, one department, or the people in one division. A company team "includes" everyone on the payroll. Anyone that isn't important to the company shouldn't be on the payroll. Managers make a serious mistake when they fail to consider that everyone employed by the company is a valuable member of the same master team.

Street Smart Managers follow an inclusive process of team building. They know that the real company team is made up of every single employee of the company.

Most corporate employees will never be responsible for leading an entire company. More than likely, most people will start out leading a smaller team within a larger team. As managers advance up the corporate ladder, they will then be charged with leading larger and larger teams, usually made up of lots of smaller teams.

Teams come in all shapes and sizes. I call the most common of all teams:

Tiny Teams.

Tiny Teams consist of the smallest numbers of people making up a team, working closely together on a regular basis. Tiny Teams are just two people, working one-with-one.

Bosses and their personal assistants make up one of the basic Tiny Teams.

Salespeople are on Tiny Teams with each of their individual customers. A purchasing agent and a supplier merge into a Tiny Team. Tiny Teams are everywhere.

Two person relationships form the basic building blocks of all teamwork, in every single aspect of life.

No matter what calling you have in life, teamwork holds the key to success. Even hermits have to rely on teamwork, because the rest of the people have to agree to leave a hermit alone.

People who love themselves, and who love others enough to create and maintain happy, workable, trusting, one-on-one relationships, have already mastered the real secret to a life of lasting success.

People who have a healthy love for themselves have no trouble loving others, and they can allow themselves to be loved by others. They serve others, and they graciously accept being served by others as well. These are truly happy people.

Look at life though dark colored glasses and you will see a stressful and foreboding scene. View life as sunny and bright, and you'll think life is a picnic.

Most people create their own obstacles along the toll-free road to success. They take endless detours that keep them running off of the roadway. They get distracted by fear, and they worry over things that they can't control, overlooking the important things that they can control.

Unhappiness and frustration comes from feeling like you're stuck in the same spot forever. It's like taking a step in the right direction with your left foot, but never following up with a step in the same direction with your right foot. You haven't moved forward at all.

Why is your individual happiness so important to your success in the business world? I think the answer is quite obvious and very practical. I haven't found anybody yet who likes to work with a mean, loud, frustrated, obnoxious, defensive, crude, complaining, and depressing person. So, have fun and remember this thought:

Happiness is Success!

If, you have opened to this book to the last few pages before reading the first pages, perhaps you will clearly understand the complete meaning and wisdom of my two-step theory of success without going back to read the beginning chapters. It's a very simple concept.

On the other hand, if you want some added insight as to how and why my Street Smart formula works, I think that you'll find the entire book to be interesting, easy to read, and easy to understand. I hope you'll read it and enjoy it.

For those readers who are anxious to instantly start down the real road to fulfillment, here it is, as promised. It only takes these two small steps to get on the straight road to happiness and success:

Step One — Love Yourself
Step Two — Serve Others

That's all it takes. However, please remember this:

You must take both steps in the same direction in order to avoid turning around and around in the same spot.

If these two steps along the road to happiness don't bring you the "Success" you deserve, I suggest that you bring your complaint to God. After all, He's the one that created us the way we are.

Key Word Index

Authority, 45

Compatibility, 244

Delegation, 208

Dialogue Direction, 105

Empowerment, 199

Five Knows, 186

Four C Club, 102

Fun/Stress Factor, 24

Loyalty Ladder, 191

Management styles, 24, 25

Planning/Problem Solving, 147

Analyzing Early Signs, 174

Building Your Facts, 177

Connections, 180

Deterrents, 181

Sense of Success, 15

Street Smart Management, 25, 26

Teamwork, 229

TMPT, 152

SUGGESTED SELF-HELP READINGS

Baer, Earl E. (1975).The sensitive I. USA: John Wiley & Sons, Inc.

Baty, Gordon B. (1990). <u>Entrepreneurship for the nineties.</u> Englewood Cliffs: Prentice-Hall Inc.

Blackler, F.H.M. (1984).<u>Applying psychology in organizations</u>. USA: Methuen & Co.

Bolton, Robert (1984). <u>Social style/management style.</u> New York: American Management Associations.

Carvell, Fred J. (1975). <u>Human relations in business.</u> New York: Macmillan publishing Co., Inc.

Evered, James F. (1981). <u>Shirt-sleeves management.</u> New York: AMACON.

Gardner, James E. (1980). <u>Training the new supervisor.</u> New York: AMACOM.

Hirschhorn, Larry (1991). <u>Managing in the new team environment: skills, tools, and methods</u>. USA: Addison-Wesley Publishing Company, Inc.

Johnson, Perry L. (1993). <u>ISO 9000: Meeting the new international standards.</u> USA: McGraw-Hill, Inc.

Katzenbach, Jon R., Douglas K. Smith (1993). The wisdom of teams: creating the high performance organization. USA: McKinsey & Company, Inc.

Kinlaw, Dennis C. (1991). Developing superior work teams: building quality and the competitive edge. USA: Lexington Books.

Kipling, Rudyard (1925). Rudyard Kipling's Verse. Garden City: Doubleday, Page & Company.

Osgood, William R. (1981). Basics of successful business management. New York: AMACOM.

Reddin, W.J. (1970). Effective Management by Objectives, the 3-D method of MBO. New York: McGraw-Hill Book Company.

Robbins, Stephen P. (1994). MANAGEMENT: Concepts and Practices. Englewood Cliffs: Prentice-Hall, Inc.

White, Richard M, Jr. (1977). The entrepreneur's manual. Radnor: Chilton Book Company.

Matthew, Mark, Luke, and John (Last names unknown) New Testament, Various places, A long time ago.

www.ingramcontent.com/pod-product-compliance
Lightning Source LLC
LaVergne TN
LVHW051458080426
835509LV00017B/1801